PUL

SPEAKING

Bring Your Social Skills and Self Esteem to
the Next Level

(Improve Self Confidence and Empathy by
Mastering Your Communication Skills)

Grant Mazur

Published by Rob Miles

© **Grant Mazur**

All Rights Reserved

Public Speaking: Bring Your Social Skills and Self Esteem to the Next Level (Improve Self Confidence and Empathy by Mastering Your Communication Skills)

ISBN 978-1-989990-13-1

Legal & Disclaimer

The information contained in this book is not designed to replace or take the place of any form of medicine or professional medical advice. The information in this book has been provided for educational and entertainment purposes only.

The information contained in this book has been compiled from sources deemed reliable, and it is accurate to the best of the Author's knowledge; however, the Author cannot guarantee its accuracy and validity and cannot be held liable for any errors or omissions. Changes are periodically made to this book. You must consult your doctor or get professional medical advice before using any of the suggested remedies, techniques, or information in this book.

Table of Contents

Introduction

There will always come the time when we need to speak in front of a crowd. Public speaking is an essential part of letting our voices be heard. Whether it's a small group or a huge audience you're speaking in front of, you must be well prepared to let everyone know and understand what message it is that you wish to relay.

However, not everyone is able to speak in front of the public. There are a lot of difficulties that are present in public speaking, some of which are present in specific individuals, particularly those with stage fright, but may not occur with others. Some individuals are rather adept or they just have it in them to speak without fear or anxiety.

Public speaking could be done properly or we can do it badly. The outcome always greatly influences the way people look at the speaker or how they

1

perceive the persons thoughts and behaviors.

It is essential to take precautionary measures before publicly speaking. From the way you dress down to the very movement of your fingers, everything must be accounted for. Not a single detail must be overlooked.

Being a part of the listening crowd is somewhat a practice that we have all been living with. However, being the person on stage having to be heard by many people is like living in an entirely different world. You'd probably encounter a different perspective of things when you're up on that stage conveying your message.

Chapter 1: History Of Public Speaking

Almost three thousand years ago, public speaking as an art was born. Its roots can be traced back to formal public inquiries that served as a training ground for citizens of Greece and Rome. This way, they were able to participate in the affairs of the state. In that particular period, there was a prevailing belief that a person's capability to speak in front of a large audience is a sign that he could be utilized by the society in promoting common good and in communicating the path to progress.

To better appreciate public speaking and to orient you on the path that you should follow if you are serious with your goal of inspiring others, here is a walk through in the molders of public speaking as an art and why it is, up until today, a relevant art for communicating change and obtaining the aims of the society:

The Classical Period (500-400 BCE)

This was the time when it was realized that public speaking is an essential tool for participating in public political affairs. This period gave birth to the most important rhetoricians of all time – Aspasia, Socrates, Plato, and the popular Aristotle.

Aspasia of Miletus (469 BCE)

Regarded as the mother of rhetoric, Aspasia of Miletus was believed to be the one to teach Socrates about rhetoric. In his time, the Athenian ruler Pericles (the partner of Aspasia) treated her as an equal. Being an empowered woman, she was given the opportunity to talk with men of education and men who belonged to the higher echelons of the society. This is how she learned about rhetoric in her own simple way.

Socrates (469-399 BCE)

Socrates, on the other hand, was considered as the teacher who had the biggest influence to the direction of the Classical Period. Though his works were not able to survive the test of time, we learned more about him through Plato's writings. Plato happened to be Socrates' student.

Plato (429-347 BCE)

Plato had the opportunity to write about rhetoric through his dialogues. In his dialogues, his teacher, Socrates, was the main character. In his writings, Plato was able to lay down the foundation of rhetoric by identifying its scope. The scope of the art became more pronounced because of his negative opinions and points of view about rhetoric. Also, he gave criticisms against the Sophists because, according to him, what they taught is not about Rhetoric as an art to discover the truth. Instead, they taught how it can be used as an instrument for deceit and manipulation.

Aristotle (384-322 BCE)

Aristotle, no doubt, was most famous among the Scholars of Greece. He was the one responsible for defining what rhetoric is. In one of his famous lectures, he said the rhetoric is human kind's tool that can be utilized in discovering every plausible methodology to persuade any kind of audience in relation to a chosen topic or subject. He shared that in order to persuade, one has to know his audience first. He popularized the persuasion methods which is still popular until today: the ethos (or ethics and character of the speaker), the pathos (or the speaker's emotional aspect), and the logos (or the reasoning power or logic used by the speaker).

The Sophists (400 BCE)

The Classical Period was able to thrive for almost a thousand years in Greece. This paved the way for the establishment of a strong foundation for democracy. With the constant practice and application of rhetoric, democracy became stronger and it became more and more widely accepted. The Sophists of this period were the ones responsible for teaching ordinary citizens the art and science of public speaking. They are usually self-proclaimed teachers and professors who taught mainly about the path towards succeeding in the Greek states' civic way of living.

Cicero (106-43 BCE)

Cicero was immortalized in a sense because of his greatness as a rhetorician. In fact, he is still being regarded as one of the most important and significant rhetorician of all time. He was the one who devised a system called the Five Canons of Rhetoric. The Five Canons of Rhetoric, in simple terms, refer to a particular process that any speaker has to follow if he intends to persuade or move or affect his audience. Just like Aristotle's persuasion methods, Cicero's Five Canons of Rhetoric is still being passed on to students of modern rhetoric and speech communication in universities today.

Quintilian (35-95 CE)

Quintilian had a very peculiar claim: that the art of public speaking should be considered as a moral. Though peculiar, his claim makes sense. According to him, if you want to be an orator, you should be a man of dignity, integrity, and reputation. Speaking well is just a consequent and it is just a secondary requirement for orators.

The Medieval Period (400-1400 CE)

However, there was a shift of focus in the Medieval Period. If the Classical Period was a venue for continuous growth in communication, the Medieval Period was seen as the dark era for communication studies. It is even dubbed as the "Dark Ages" for studying public speaking. Among the reasons were the church's stance against works of rhetoric that might go against their goals. Also, the church mentioned that there might be speeches that have pagan content. But, the church used rhetoric as an aid to improve their preaching and to enhance their power to persuade the general public.

St. Augustine (354-430 CE)

St. Augustine was a clergy man and he was a famous rhetorician. He was known for following the line of thought that started in the Classical Period. He gave a significant portion of his time studying the art and method of persuasion. This proves to be an endeavor that is treasured by the church.

The Renaissance Period (1400-1600 CE)

The Renaissance Period fueled a new form of intellectual movement. During this time, the government, alongside many secular institutions began to go head to head against the church when it comes to getting a significant amount of followers. People during this period gave attention to learning how to speak in particular situations in order to communicate particular ideas.

Petrus Ramus (1515 to 1572)

Petrus Ramus gave particular attention to developing a particular style of delivering thoughts and ideas. He thought that it is not just about the content when it comes to persuasion. He believed that style counts to make the ideas more palatable for the intended audience. He also was the pioneer of the argument that arrangement and invention should not be the concern of rhetoric. Instead, he suggested that these are areas that should be turned over to logic. He challenged many notions raised during the Classical Period.

Francis Bacon (1561 to 1626)

Francis Bacon lived during Shakespeare's time. He expressed his belief that the path towards the truth should be the primary concern of communication. According to him, morality and reason compels a speaker to be accountable. Therefore, accountability and sense of responsibility are two important elements of oration.

The Era of Enlightenment (1600-1800)

The classical approach of Rhetoric was revived and it was adapted in the contemporary context. Hence, this era was also called the era of Neoclassicism.

George Campbell (1719 to 1796)

George Campbell was an educator and minister. He attempted to make arguments by utilizing moral and scientific reasoning. He made significant efforts to further understand the way individuals made use of public speaking to convince others to share their stance on issues. He focused on the use of proper delivery and style. He called it the elocutionary approach. Here, strict rules on facial expressions, gestures, pronunciation, and tone were given. Also, during this period, a branch known to be "political rhetoric" was born due to the birth of American Revolution and French Revolution.

The American Revolution

During this period, studying Roman and Greek Rhetoric was a major effort. In this period, efforts to revive speeches from famous and significant Roman and Greek rhetoricians were made. The teachers in this period give much emphasis on the teachings and the works of Aristotle as well as that of Cicero. John Quincy Adams of the Harvard University asserted that further efforts should be given and exerted to develop and teach the art of rhetoric.

The 20th Century Efforts

This is a mere continuation of past efforts to develop and teach rhetoric as a major field of study. In many universities, colleges, and schools around the globe, public speaking courses were offered. In these higher courses, the Greeks' fundamental theories of thinking and speaking were widely applied. The models of persuasion and the Canons of Rhetoric were taught, together with other concepts.

In the 1960s and 1970s, the emphasis on works from the Classical Period was renewed. These decades served as a bridge to fill the gap between Communication Study's old school and new school. For the first time, rhetoric was taught in complementation with contemporary rhetoric, classical rhetoric, qualitative social sciences, and empirical sciences.

Chapter 2: Gauging Your Anxiety

Before diving into any form of anxiety treatment, you should first figure out the depth of your anxiety. It's time to get that heart to heart talk with yourself and figure out how deep is your fear of public speaking. If you can do it and only have a mild case of apprehension (perhaps with a few squeaks in your voice, a bit of sweating, and some shaking of the hands that everyone can see) then you don't have to worry about any serious anxiety issues.

Remember: It's okay to be a little nervous about any speech you have to give in a public engagement. At least you know you're human. It's a very human response and its okay. You know why? Because everyone gets a little excited about a talk or speech they have to give. You're excited about your speech and it simply means that you care about it.

What If it's More Serious than You Think?

Now, how do you know if you're dealing with more than just a case of cold feet about giving a speech to a room full of guests? It's time to look a little deeper then. Try to answer the following questions below as honestly as you can. The answers may help you understand how you really feel about speaking engagements.

Question #1 – How long did you worry about your speaking engagement? A week? Two weeks? An entire month?

How far away in advance were you told about your speaking engagement? Did they tell you about it a month before? Or did they tell you that you have to give a talk in the next five minutes.

Now besides the length of time you spent worrying about your upcoming speech, try to gauge how worried were you about it. Were there times when you couldn't eat or sleep? Did it make you worry insomuch that it interfered with your daily routine? If you worried so much about your speech that it interfered with your daily routine then that may be a sign of something more serious.

Question #2 – How negative were your thoughts?

Try to evaluate how your thoughts were when you were worried about your speaking engagement. How did you feel about yourself while being introduced to the audience? Did you worry about saying something stupid? Did you worry about anyone noticing that your voice was shaky? Did you worry whether you looked good or not?

Do these negative thoughts come to your mind automatically without warning? Do you have a hard time keeping them out of your head? If these negative thoughts can go out of control insomuch that you have shut out the world around you then you may be facing something more serious.

Question #3 — How often have you avoided speaking engagements?

Now we're going through the motions a little bit deeper. Were there other speaking engagements that you avoided? Did you give an excuse so that you won't have to give a speech or did you just not show up on the appointed day? People who have a much serious type of anxiety will usually avoid any form of speaking engagements.

Remember that this can happen to students as well as professionals. There are students who select their coursework that requires fewer presentations. There are students who shift and jump from one course to another in an effort to avoid presentations. There are also professionals who turn down a promotion simply because the new job post requires some form of speaking obligation.

After answering these questions if you feel that you have a serious issue with or an uncontrollable fear of public speaking then it would be a good idea to get help. Those who have manageable symptoms can overcome their public speaking anxiety with the help of books like this one. They can be managed easily using the tips and exercises which you will learn later in this book.

Glossophobia and SAD

Glossophobia is one of the most usual social fears that people experience. However, as indicated in the questions above, when the symptoms of such fears have become so intense that it affects the way an individual make decisions and interferes with one's normal life then they may be a sign that an individual has some form of social anxiety disorder. The American Psychiatric Association has published a diagnostic manual to help mental health workers identify actual cases of SAD and differentiate it from other symptoms.

Obviously, you can't diagnose SAD unless you are a trained mental health professional. In order to diagnose if a person does have social anxiety disorder or not, certain criteria should be met. Using their manual of mental health disorders, mental health professionals will ask questions to help determine a person's actual condition.

Some of the questions will probe the physical symptoms that a person experiences when giving a speech or some other stressful social situations. There will also be questions that will gauge how persistent and how significant is that fear that a person experiences. Some questions will determine whether a person can recognize just how unreasonable their rationalizations are. Finally, some questions will determine a person's reaction to such stressful situations – whether they will avoid it or just endure it.

When a person is diagnosed as having fear toward one or a handful of perceived intense social situations then that individual may be diagnosed with a condition that experts call as Specific SAD. Now, if a person tends to fear and avoid every single form of social situations then that person may be diagnosed with Generalized SAD.

Where to Find Help When You Need It

Remember that help is always available when you need it. In case that you feel that you have more serious symptoms of presentation anxiety then get help as soon as possible. The sooner you deal with the issue the easier it will be for you in the end. You will be helping no one else but yourself.

If you have insurance then you may contact the insurance company and ask for recommendations. You may also contact your state's psychiatric association. If you're a student you may contact your school's psychology department for counseling or at least a referral. Another option is to ask family and friends if they can recommend a doctor, mental health worker, or mental health organization.

Chapter 3: Know Your Reason For Being.

Every presentation has a purpose. The more you understand about exactly why you are getting up in front of a group of people to talk to them, the easier it will be for you to stay focused. The reason we are making this the first step in your preparation to put together a dynamite talk is that the core goal of the presentation will dictate what goes into your outline, how you do your research, how to use humor if it is appropriate and every other aspect about your moment of public speaking.

Your audience may know full well why you are there. They will evaluate how well your presentation goes based on how well you meet that goal as well. Of course, you have your own goals but those are your own and secondary to the reason for the talk.

You want to be liked, to see your presentation go off without a hitch and maybe even be asked back to speak to that group again. You will accomplish those goals with your presentation style which we will discuss more about in a little bit.

There are four basic types of public speaking scenarios and each one has a different goal that you will be targeting when you research and write your speech and when you deliver it. It is good to understand these four basic speech types so you can categorize your talk and focus your approach on reaching that goal.

Public Speaking to Inform

Often your goal of your presentation is to teach your audience about the subject matter of the presentation. Teachers or other educators have this focus and success is achieved when the audience goes away knowing more about the topic at hand than when they came.

It is often difficult to determine if you have been successful in achieving that goal because learning doesn't show on the outside. That is where including some form of interaction such as a question and answer period at the end of your talk will help you to know if you have been a success.

It might seem that when you are preparing your presentation with a goal of informing or teaching your audience, you can get away with "just the facts." That temptation will often result in a boring presentation which defeats the purpose. So to be a success, you should still plan on making your talk interesting, amusing, fun and challenging with lots of chances for the audience to let you know that they are staying with you.

Public Speaking to Amuse

If your goal during your time in front of an audience is simply to amuse, your focus is not as much on content. The content can be jokes, story telling or humorous observations. A roast environment where you and friends are lovingly mocking someone is that kind of presentation. However, just because your only goal is to get some smiles on the faces of your audience, that does not reduce the stress. To be a success, think about your style and timing as much as about what you have to say.

A speech given to amuse will still have an outline with a beginning, several points in the middle and a conclusion. Do not fall into the trap of not preparing for such a moment of public speaking. Nothing will harm your ability to amuse others more than anxiousness when you stand up to deliver your talk.

Public Speaking to Reflect or Inspire

This is actually one of the most common types of public speaking events that you may be called upon to be part of. It includes things such as giving a toast at a wedding or funeral or speaking in a religious service.

A speech given to inspire does not have to educate but it might reveal to the audience or congregation revelations that are new such as a religious observation. In a way, a public speaking event that is there to inspire has elements of both instructional and persuasive speech because often the goal of such a presentation is to inspire action or change of behavior in the listener.

Public Speaking to Persuade

Persuasive public speaking may be the most common kind that you may be called upon to deliver. Public speaking events in business or sales contexts are almost always designed to "close the deal". Usually political speeches are designed to change the way the audience views a subject and as such, they are persuasive in nature.

A public speaking situation that has a goal of persuading combines the emotional and logical sides of the listener's personality. You will build an argument for why your point of view is the right one. There is often an educational side to a persuasive speech as you bring the audience up to speed on the facts of the situation being addressed. But even then, how you present those facts and the facts you pick to present are organized in a way to contribute to the final goal which is to talk the audience into becoming part of your movement or agreeing with your goals that you are presenting in your talk.

There are lots of situations that will come up where you will suddenly be called upon to deliver a speech. Extemporaneous public speaking happens when you give a speech without a formal outline. If you find yourself facing an audience to give an ad hoc speech, simply think about what the goal of the presentation is and address that goal.

If you are talking to the group to inform, call upon your existing knowledge to accomplish that goal. If your goal is to reflect, call upon your memories of the event or person to find something nostalgic for your subject matter. If your goal is to persuade, look within yourself for the passion you have for that topic and find a way to make your audience just as passionate as you are. If your goal is to amuse, resort to that natural charm you have and share that with the world.

You can do your homework on the goals of your talk when you are given the opportunity to speak to a group. Often the organization or person who offers you the chance to speak to a group will have an agenda. Armed with what you now know about the different kinds of speeches that are given, you can pose the question openly about whether your talk should be designed to educate, to inform, to inspire or to entertain. While it may have elements of several of these public speaking goals, there is always one ruling objective and that is the one you want as your goal. You are ahead of the game if you know that goal before you write the first word of the speech that you will give.

Chapter 4: The Art Of Speaking In

Public

Becoming involved in a public speaking club called Rostrum (the British version of Toastmasters) for many years I watched many great speakers and learn what makes a good speaker. In the chapter below, I have listed those strategies that I feel apply to a public speaking situation and are important for those new to public speaking to know for them to become good speakers. They are:-

1.Make sure there is light on your face for your audience to see your lips and facial expressions. Your facial expressions add meaning and emphasis to what you say.

2.Don't shout when you are in a public speaking situation. However, add colour to your voice. Use pause or slow down or speed up your words or raise or lower your voice to create a feeling of importance in what you are saying or about to say.

3.Speak more slowly when giving a speech. It should be slower than your normal conversational speech. This allows the audience more time to absorb the meaning of what you are saying.

4.Avoid noisy backgrounds. This distracts the audience from what you say and lessens their concentration.

5.Get the point across quickly. Don't over explain a new idea.

6.Use the 'Kiss' principle: 'Keep it simple, stupid'.

7.Be enthusiastic as you give your speech. Show you love to speak and you want your audience to enjoy the experience.

8.Watch your audience closely and react to their body language as it will tell you how successful you are with your presentation.

9.Get the attention of your audience with a strong or interesting or controversial opening.

10.Use body language, facial expressions and gesture to help to get your message across and to emphasise the important points or issues.

11.If you are nervous, take a few deep breaths before you start. This nervousness may occur early in your speaking career or when you are giving an important speech. However, once the speech gets underway, this nervousness will disappear.

12.If you are about to forget a point or have made a mistake in your presentation, just keep going. No one in the audience knows what you are going to say. So they won't know you have made a mistake or forgotten a point unless you make them aware of it by stopping or apologising.

13.Sometimes you pause because you have forgotten what comes next and then suddenly you remember. So just keep going with the speech. You might think you have paused for a 'long' time but in reality it is really short. It seems long because your mind moves many times faster than your voice. In practicing your speech you will come to realise the parts of the speech that are 'accident' prone. So prepare a strategy to cover the event e. g. a gesture; a dramatic pause...

In conclusion, remember your voice is your greatest asset. You must look after it. If you have trouble with using your voice effectively in public, seek professional advice and training. A professional will explain to you the mechanics of your voice; teach you how to breathe and how to project.

Chapter 5: Chatty Cathy

Heather Penn

Topic: Icebreaker designed to promote early group communication.

Learning Objectives: This learning activity is designed to:
•Engage students immediately
•Encourage positive communication early in the term
•Enhance views of equality as everyone follows the same path.

Description of Activity: This activity includes two students (dyad) and a list of questions. The students have two minutes to chat with their partner, then they must stand up and give a summary of the person they have just met with one false fact thrown in for fun. This activity provides students with the opportunity to meet other students right away and foster a sense of community. Moreover, this activity promotes interpersonal and group communication skills they will develop over the course of the semester. Additionally, this gives the professor insight on student interests, providing an opportunity to pick relevant content throughout the semester to promote student engagement.

Materials needed: No supplemental material is necessary.

Prep time for students: This is a timed activity for the student and is usually done the first day of class. Students are given two minutes to meet their partner then they must give a brief summary on the person they just met. Notes are allowed

Assignment time: 6 minutes total; 2 minutes per student to speak with their partner and ask their questions, then 1 minute per student to share their partners' mini biography.

Instructions for Instructor: On the first day of class, wait until all the students are in their seats and have them turn to their left. If there is a left-over student, they may pair up with the instructor and

utilize the same protocol. The students then have 2 minutes to ask as much about their partner as they can.

They may take notes. You will be timing the interview portion, ensuring the time of two minutes is accurate. Once the two-minute timer is up for each student, the students draw on the information gathered and take turns (at the front of the class) introducing the person they just interviewed to include one made up fact about the interviewee. The made-up fact cannot be hurtful. The class then decides which statement from the interview is false. This allows the entire class to get in on the activity and engage with the entire class. Play continues until everyone has been introduced.

Instructions for Student: Class, we are going to pair up and get to know each other. Look to your left. Make eye contact with your peer. This is your partner for this learning activity. Go ahead and move. Face each other.

(After the class has settled...) I will set a timer for two minutes at which time you will begin interviewing your neighbor to get their likes, interests, etc. Sample questions may include the following:

•Where were you born?

•How did you end up in Alaska?

•What major or interests are you pursuing?

•What are your hobbies?

•Where is the coolest place you've ever visited and why?

•Encourage students to get creative.

Please do not follow these exact questions and call it done. Be creative. Try to get something more interesting than just "this is Amy, and she is a bio major." Help us get to know your peers. And, be respectful when asking questions. Don't get too personal.

You are looking for: Brief history as you need to find out enough about your peer to stand up and give the class a brief summary. Your neighbor will stand up and do the same thing.

One more thing. Don't forget to throw in a false statement. This statement can be anything, such as "Amy is an avid fan of Pokémon." Keep it simple and clean.

Necessary Background: Many times, the first day of school can be very nerve-wracking. This activity places an immediate demand to meet and interact with someone and then turn around and introduce them as well as make up a fun fact. A clear understanding of what the class content entails is established almost immediately.

Debrief: To debrief we would examine the student's reactions to the activity handed down. Topics for discussion may include the following:

•What body language, eye contact, avoidance attributes helped identify the false statement?

•Was it hard to speak for 1 minute?

•Allow students the opportunity to reflect on anxiety and overall level of comfort with the public speaking process.

•What factors contributed to student engagement?

Variations: Drop the false statement and stick with a basic introduction.

Trouble spots: Students will use the list of sample questions provided and contribute nothing original. Some students may knowingly ask offensive questions, or we get the same question and answers over and over again. Encourage students to be creative.

Common questions students ask:

•How long do I have to talk? Answer: One minute.

•Do I have to get up in front of the class? Answer: Yes. This is a public speaking class. You will be in front of the class all term.

Chapter 6: What The Gutsy Girls Pocket

Guide Is All About

This book isn't just for the person who wants to be a speaker; it's for the person who is called to speak. You may be the CEO of your company and want to learn how to be more impactful from the podium. Maybe you're the owner of a home-based business, and you are realizing that your ability to close sales and generate income is a direct reflection of your ability to communicate with power. Maybe you're a sales person who wants to close more sales. Or maybe you've got a burning desire to be the voice for those who have no voice – to speak on behalf of a cause or a charity. There are many avenues out there where women are called to step up and speak out. And, as you know, speaking in public is not always easy or desirable. In fact, for some people it is downright terrifying.

So this book is for you. This book is not for the professional speaker (although I think it may hold value for you too) but for the person who is called to speak and doesn't do it by trade. You've come to the right place. We'll put your fears to rest and help you conquer the stage and get the most power from your voice.

I wrote this book for women because I know that we're different from men. Equal, yes. But different. We bring a different set of fears, anxieties, gifts, talents, and issues than men. And I wanted this book to be just for us. But if you're a man reading this – you are just as welcome - and all the power to you for getting in touch with your feminine side. Good move. Being able to impact women will serve you well. So carry this pink book with pride.

Why Gusty?

I call this book a "gutsy" guide because I am calling you to be bold. Speaking in public is not for the timid. Sharing your story takes confidence. It involves coming out of your comfort zone. So I'm going to push you beyond the status quo. I'm going to push you out of the chorus line and into the spotlight. That's where the true impact lies.

There are plenty of people in the "chorus line" of speaking. They are the ones who dress alike, talk alike, follow the same script, and are basically interchangeable. And they're the ones nobody really notices or remembers. And often their message goes unheard. They are a commodity. This is not where we want to be. We want to be the ones who stand out, who make a difference, who are remembered long after we are gone. Our message is too important to get lost in the shuffle. It's simple to get out of the chorus line. Not easy. Just simple. And you can do it. If you're willing to be gutsy.

Why Girls?

You might be wondering why I created a book just for women. Wouldn't men find these tips helpful too? You bet. But women are different from men. We relate to the world differently. We relate to each other differently. We bring a different set of gifts and a different set of anxieties. The world still , to some degree , treats women differently. So , until that changes, I wanted something just for us.

And men, if you are reading this, all the power to you. You're just as welcome. And kudos for being bold enough to carry around a pink book for girls.

Why Pocket Guide?

Let's face it, we're all busy. And while there are tons of good books out there, many of us simply don't have time to read them. I have a stack of books sitting beside my bed that haven't even been opened. Sometimes I just need someone to give me the facts. I don't want to wade through a bunch of text and stories to get there. I just need the information.

That's what this book is — the information — mixed in with a little personality so it won't be mind-numbingly boring. So occasionally I will throw in a little chuckle, or some words of inspiration. But other than that, this is just a pocket guide - bullet points to help you give your speech a makeover and to help you claim your place in the spotlight where you belong.

Chapter 7: The Goals Of Public

Speaking

Anyone who is going to speak to a group of people must have specific goals in mind. You need to know what you are trying to achieve, what the audience would like to hear, and what you want to get out of the speaking experience.

Whenever you speak to people, the goals you are attempting to achieve are to verbally express your thoughts and ideas, satisfy the listeners or audience, and get rewards from the process.

So take your time to find out what you want out of the presentation and what your audience may also want. Before you can go any further, you must figure these out. Generally, most presentations will fall into one of the following two types:

Informative: A presentation that introduces a new subject or reexamines a familiar one. When you are addressing the attendees of a comic book convention about the history of Batman, your intent is to inform and present the facts about the Caped Crusader in as objective a manner as possible.

Persuasive: A presentation designed to change the listeners' views and/or actions. If, at that same convention, you are asked to speak on Why Batman Would Win in a Battle against the Incredible Hulk, your mission is to present a clear opinion on the subject and convince your audience that you are correct. Both of these approaches have their benefits.

Without a keen awareness of what you want to say and how you want to say it, at minimum you will leave your audience unimpressed. At worst, you may accidentally let slip information you didn't mean to share.

Although your presentation will have much of the same information whether you mean to inform or persuade, you must follow through with one approach or the other. Starting off a presentation in an informative way and then switching to a persuasive tone halfway through will confuse your audience and waste time. Figuring out which approach to take and sticking to it will make your presentation and the visual aids you use in it much stronger.

The message of your presentation is the line you would blurt out if you only had five seconds of time with your listener. You should be able to write the message you want to convey as a simple sentence. Spend a good amount of time refining your message as you prepare your preparation because, it is the main point your listeners will take with them and so you must make it a good one.

What Do You Want To Achieve?

Before you give a speech, you really need to define what you want or expect to achieve in the talk. This is really the purpose of your talk, which can be any or all of the following:

i. To Inform

ii. To Educate

iii. To Arouse

iv. To Persuade

v. To Move To Action

vi. To Entertain

It is important to make a personal statement of what you want to achieve before even starting to write your speech. For example, "In speaking to this group, I want to persuade them to consider our product, while also entertaining them with my stories."

Provide Listener Satisfaction

Speaking is a communication process. If the listener or audience does not understand or enjoy what you are saying, you have not achieved a major goal of the process.

Important factors to remember in obtaining listener satisfaction are:

i. Speak with confidence,

ii. Speak with clarity, and

iii. Get the audience to participate.

iv. Expressing your ideas

A major motivation in speaking to a group or anyone for that matter is to express your ideas. In some cases, people may actually ask you to express your thoughts on a certain subject.

It is sometimes difficult to verbally express what you are thinking to other people. Those without the "gift of rattle-on" may have trouble putting their thoughts into words or may even fear speaking to others or to a group. Even professional speakers occasionally come down with the anxieties before giving a speech.

Organize Your Thoughts

You should organize your thoughts before speaking to a group or on a one-to-one basis with a superior. Try to keep things down to three major points. Some people can organize what they plan to say in their heads, while most need to write things down.

There are some techniques to facilitate the verbal expression of your thoughts, such as writing and public speaking methods. Speaking well at work in presentations, at meetings or simply in personal interactions will create a better impression of your competence and result in raises and promotions.

Professional Speaking

Some speakers are good enough to charge money for their skills. At the local level, a speaker may receive $25 to speak to a Local Club. At the top end, celebrity speakers can receive $100,000 for a half-hour speech.

Professional speakers fall into three categories: those that have a good message, those that are entertaining or eloquent speakers, and those who are famous or celebrities. The famous speakers are the ones that get paid the most for their presence and words. A successful speaker achieves the goals of expression, listener satisfaction and desired rewards. You should be aware

of your goals as you pursue success in
speaking.

Chapter 8: What Will You Learn?

For the purposes of this book, I consider the following occasions are 'public speaking' events.

•Those horrible around the table introductions at meetings

•'Thank You' speeches at birthdays, anniversaries, award nights, etc.

•Wedding speeches

•Delivering training

•Role playing at a training course (ugh)

•Getting attention from a customer service person

•Job interviews

•Performance reviews

•And, of course giving a speech in front of groups of total strangers – or worse, peers

Most public speaking courses concentrate on the last item in this list. However, I believe that many people find some or all of the others in the list just as daunting and nerve wracking.

Therefore this book addresses many of these situations.

Hopefully from my mistakes you will learn how to risk manage any situation where you are required to present in public.

And, with a little luck, planning and practice you can go from sweaty palms to relative calm.

Wardrobe malfunctions 101

It was a hot and steamy summer's day in Brisbane's western suburbs (north eastern Australia). I was about to speak in 'public' for the first time. The audience, a class of Year 11 history students, sat attentively waiting for my maiden speech. The class was eerily quiet with the fans in the room providing the only noise and spreading the thick, warm, damp air lazily around the room. The students were sitting upright with their full attention on me.

I must pause here to explain that the audience of 16 year olds were so well-behaved not because of any threat, coercion or pubescent anomaly but because they were peers and friends of my children. A late bloomer, I had decided in my 30's to become a teacher. My two children were well into high school and, although I didn't choose to do my practice teaching at their school, fate would have it that not only did I get to teach in their school but to their actual Year levels. Good grief.

I had dressed in my favourite and comfortable (but cute and fashionable) pink satin blouse and felt nervous but not terrified. I kept reminding myself to breathe.

I was about five minutes into my extensively-researched and painstakingly thorough lesson plan (see lesson 2 below) when thunder struck-literally and loudly. A sudden afternoon summer storm hit with a vengeance. The air, already high in humidity, became almost unbearable. The thunder became louder and the rain began to pelt on the tin roof. I kept talking; the students kept looking at me and participating when asked. As the atmosphere got damper so did the "underarm -soakademia". I felt the dampness rise and kept my arms close to my sides as I realised my pretty pale pink blouse was becoming darker under my arms. As my anxiousness grew so did the perspiration. Sweaty patches were appearing everywhere. I spoke louder and louder to be heard above the din. Drops of perspiration began appearing like polka dots on my blouse. I tried not to move too much lest the blouse come further in contact with my body. My first day of teaching had become more like a wet t-shirt competition!

I was so relieved when the bell went for the end of class that my head was spinning. I'd done it - it was over – except that I hadn't gotten through even half of the lesson plan.

Those wonderful children remained focused and, I swear, felt for my fairly obvious 'discomfort' – they had to if they ever wanted to be fed, housed and counselled at their friend's house ever again!

Lessons 1, 2 and 3 for risk managing public speaking events:

1.Always have a backup plan - for days of inclement weather and external interference (in this case extreme noise).

2.Less can definitely be more. Be aware of just how little information you can get through in 50 minutes.

3.Don't wear anything that shows sweat!

After the class emptied of students, my supervisor also expressed surprise that his class could be so amenable and that in all his years of teaching he had never had students respond to a student teacher's questions so politely - and use 'Mum' instead of 'Miss' when raising their hands to ask a question (and not even notice).

They are all grown up now and I hope they might now know just how much I appreciated their encouragement on that first day. Not all audiences are that kind.

Chapter 9: Preparing Your Speech And Use Of Technology

'Important' people might well have 'speech writers' to prepare their speeches for them, especially if they have several different speeches to deliver during a day. The vast majority of us, however, will have to prepare our own speeches.

Writing our own speeches is important for the following reasons:

•We have ownership of what we are going to say. This makes the speech more genuine and convincing

•The process of writing down a speech forces us to think and plan what we have to say and how to express our thoughts.

•We use our own words and expressions - not ones foisted upon us.

Our Western culture is dominated by the written word. Writing has different conventions from those used when speaking. Some characteristics of writing are that:

•The sentences we write are likely to be longer than those used when speaking.

•Paragraphs are usually longer than 'paragraphs' in speech that reflect pauses when we draw breath.

•The written form allows complex constructions within a sentence - easily understood when read - but which are too long to follow orally.

•In certain languages the written forms may be significantly different from the forms of the spoken language.

Remember that when we speak:

•Sentences are likely to be shorter than when we write. Full stops indicate pauses. Commas also usually indicate pauses that are shorter than those at the end of sentences.

•Paragraphs or blocks of speech are also relatively short compared with written texts. This allows us to take breath as we talk.

- We talk more simply than we write and avoid complicated constructions.
- The language we use might still be formal but it is colloquial.
- We avoid old-fashioned structures and vocabulary.
- Where there are differences in constructions or morphology between the written and the oral form then we use the oral rather than written ones.
- It is our tone of voice that adds emphasis or emotion to what we say rather than emphatic word order or grammatical devices.
- It will perhaps be appropriate to speak in a more localised form of speech, or in a dialect, rather than the standardised oral form of your language.

In short, members of the audience will know immediately whether you are delivering a speech or just regurgitating a written essay. Therefore it might be a good idea to stop after a couple of paragraphs, read them aloud and comply with oral requirements. It is far easier to do this in short, sharp bursts rather than leaving it all until the end.

Effective use of word processors.

Programs such as Word and Pages(Mac) are very useful for the following reasons:

•They can keep a running count of the length of what you are writing

•If you speak often in public, you can create your own standardised templates.

•Editing of material is easy. This can mean editing material you are writing for the first time or reusing and recasting material you have used previously.

•You can save documents for future use.

•Word processing allows you to change the size of the font of what you are printing. As I've got older, I've found it easier to read Arial 12 rather than Arial 10. In low light locations, I print my material in Arial 14.

•You can vary the font and 'mark up' a script/ speech in a way that is personal to you to help you with a delivery. I usually bold the main messages of my speech with the intermediate material in the normal font.

I recently glimpsed a BBC court reporter's script on screen. She was reporting on a trial. She obviously used different colours to show what needed to be emphasised. Defendants' names were clearly identified.

Note: It is not advisable to type " raise voice here", or 'pause here" in the body of your text as you may read the remark out!

For me, one of the main advantages is that the Word Processed file can often be transferred from your computer to a tablet or even to a smartphone – and this portability gives greater flexibility.

I still like a printed version of a speech on paper. I might well have a version typed on A4 paper when I know that this can be put on a lectern. I might, however, also have a version printed on A5 sheets of paper as they are more discrete. If I know that I will be standing to deliver a speech, I will print a version in A6. The sheets fit neatly into my hand and I can look down at them discretely.

If you have 'learnt' your speech, you may find that having a list of prompts is all that you need. At first, however, it is best to have a full copy of your speech to ensure that you have something to fall back on if being nervous plays havoc with your normally excellent memory!

Thinking ahead

Preachers I know keep a diary of their sermons - where and when they were delivered and the main points of their speech, if not copies of their whole sermons. This serves several purposes:

a) If you become well known for being an expert in a certain field, you are likely to be invited to deliver similar speeches on the topic. You do not want to repeat precisely the same 'sermon' to the same audience.

b) A speech that has already been written and saved on a word processor can be improved and modified for the next audience. Examples can often be updated. New anecdotes can be used which refer to more recent, possibly very topical events.

Chapter 10: Be Yourself

It is very important that you are genuine with your audience. This creates trust.

In a company, employees who fail to get the trust of the board will often be demoted or get fired. Teachers will also never get the attention of there students if they seem untrustworthy. Even the door to door salesman will never be able to make sales if they lack integrity or trust.

A key point that you need to remember when it comes to public speaking is that eye contact is crucial. Eye contact is important since it can reveal your true intentions. It fosters a sense of comfort and trust with your audience. It also relaxes you and gives you the feeling that you are simply having a conversation with your audience. It also gives you subtle feedback as to how your talk is being received and gives clues to any adjustments you will make along the way.

Remember to look at all the people who are watching you and never focus on one group or individual. If you have to look at your audience, look directly into their eyes. The proper eye contact will reveal that you are a trustworthy speaker and your listeners will surely be listening to your every word.

Next, we will be discussing your movements. Your body movements can reveal your lifestyle and attitude. People who are confident also walk with strong strides while less confident individuals tend to have their heads down. Your crowd can find out if you are confident through your body movements. You will notice that if you apply any movements which are not your own you will feel uncomfortable and appear awkward. Therefore, you need to make your movements as natural as possible. Never apply any hand gestures or head movements which are not in your normal personality. If you think that you need to apply hand movements, then practice them constantly first before you apply them to your crowd.

Finally, you also need to be yourself following your speech. Never act too friendly or too arrogant. Shake the hands of the people around you and be respectful. If you want to talk to people, never look too busy. Never talk to the crowd while on your phone. Thank them for listening to your speech and ask them about your topic. Most people might even suggest something about your speech. If you receive any negative feedback, remember to take it as a sign of improvement and be as professional as possible.

Chapter 11: Audience/Speaker

Connection

We want connection, not perfection!
One of Jack's great little sayings that you'll
Probably read way too many times in this book
Certainly, the material is important. In most cases, the "material" is the seeming reason the audience and performer end up in the same room at the same time. I can't overstate the importance of knowing your content. Command your subject, have your speech/part/routine not just committed to memory but safely tucked away in your DNA.
Having said that, let's ask ourselves what the audience really wants. You might say we want to be entertained. OK, I'll buy that. We want to learn something. Right again. We want to be

inspired. Maybe we even want to be provoked.

Those are great answers, but I say that we want to take you home. We can't tell you this, but this is it, and when you're an audience member, you want to take the performer home too. You want to walk out of the auditorium with the experience of the day tucked deep inside.

We want communion.

Content & Connection

Content said to Connection: "Without me they'd have no reason to show up."

Connection said to Content: "Without me they'd have no reason to stay."

You see, there are 2 parts to any performance: the content and the connection. Certainly, the content has to pass muster — let me say it again, there is no substitute for being prepared — but if it does, there is a possibility in live performance that doesn't quite exist anywhere else.

Communion.

The Us Bus

"Goodness, we all got on the Us Bus, and I thought we were going to drive around the block, but by the time we were done, we were flying round the world. Goodness!"

Alice, happy-but-mystified audience member

Your job as a performer is to get your audience on your bus. Help them on, point them in the right direction and get that baby moving. Once on, you can take that bus anywhere. You can take that bus through dramatic, twisting tunnels, on a joy ride, around hairy curves. If they're all on the bus and trust the driver — that's you — you can turn that bus into a Pegasus and fly us to the moon. Or to Detroit...wherever.

But first you have to get us on the bus.

An unknown standup comedian has 30 seconds or less to get an audience on his bus. He has to establish his point of view, the hook of his humor and he has to indicate where the audience is supposed to laugh. A speaker has about the same amount of time. Whether it's fair or not, audiences make quick judgments about the credibility and authority of a speaker. First impressions count. (If you don't create a good first impression, it could end up being your last one.

Cliché

The best and the worst performers have a cliché. Your cliché represents your present combination of ease and comfort as a performer, your skills level and your natural tribe (the types of people who most easily tune into you).

Comfort Zone.

No matter how rich, how poor, how strong, how weak... as human beings we have at least one thing in common: we all live in our own comfort zones. And, in these comfort zones, we are lords and masters. This is our domain. Here we are sovereign. This is where we feel at ease. For some of us, it's very small. Perhaps the only place where we feel truly comfortable is in our bedroom, in bed, lights out, covers tucked tightly under chin, Letterman on, a bag of potato chips at our side.

Others have much more expanded comfort zones. We're at ease with young people, old people, in new situations, in front of an audience, etc.

Whoever we are, we've already arranged our lives to keep out what we don't want to confront and to keep in what we think we can handle.

This is not to say all is rosy in our comfort zones. We have our soap operas... but it's our soap opera, our drama, our angst... and, in its way, it's safe. We know it. We've been through it thousands of times before. We always pull out.

The operable point is this: Our performance abilities are directly related to these comfort zones. If you're at ease in front of an audience and able to be in the present, the rest is a piece of cake (or a piece of pie, as my then-

Swedish wife used to say). If we're not so comfortable, the task is to raise our comfort levels.

That's what our work is all about.

Skills level.

An audience wants a powerful experience of you. The most important aspect of that experience is a comfortable, authentic "you" in front of us. However, once you're comfortable enough bringing your essence forth, a few theatrical skills can go a long way. Inflection, dramatic tone, gestures and mannerisms, vocal range...these kinds of things.

This is also what the work is about.

Tribe.

Your inherent style and approach appeals to a certain type of audience member. These are the people who resonate most naturally with you. All well and good, but if you want to include more folks on your bus, you have to expand your comfort zone and embrace them in.

In my case, as I look back on it now, I had a challenging time getting alpha males and ultra-feminine women on my bus. My natural style was more appealing to folks who appreciated my kind of off-the-wall, colloquial, quasi-alpha, high-energy style. I was not really connecting with the sprites and goddesses out there in pink, purple and mauve. They were more interested in drawing angel cards than listening to what I had to say. Same with alpha males. There was an unsaid competition for territorial domination. I'm surprised one of them didn't get up and pee around the room. Of course, I wasn't truly conscious of this at the time, but in hindsight I can see a pattern.

I had to make a conscious effort to understand what these people wanted before I could include them. I had to open my heart and have a serious talk with my ego. It was up to me, not them, to create a bigger space of understanding and compassion. If they

were going to get on the bus, I had to
give them a helping hand up.

Chapter 12: The Worst Mistakes To Make And A Few Other Pretty Bad Ones

Have you ever listened to a speaker that angered an audience? Probably not. That's because it's hard to actually do so. You might think, "Well, wouldn't it be easy if you just insulted the audience?" Not so fast there. Making fun of an audience or insulting them might actually make them laugh because they might think you're trying to be funny.

There is one way, however, to anger an audience to the point where they are almost angered. It happens all the time. How? Simple. Just listen to any speaker that fails to pause in between sentences, haven't you ever had a teacher or public speaker speak to an audience in a fast manner, and decides for some unknown reason to never,

ever pause? If you have before, how did that speaker make you feel? Were you annoyed? Probably. Did you think they deserved to get slapped? Probably. Did you lose respect for that person? Probably. I am about to teach you a little about the art of the pause, which is one of the fundamentals of public speaking.

The pause is one of the most crucial aspects of public speaking that you absolutely must incorporate into your speech. Do not make the biggest mistakes that some speakers neglect, which is to never pause. Think about it. If someone was trying to explain something complicated to you, do you think it's a good idea for them to speak continuously without ever pausing? No.

Pause between sentences. Preferably once every two or three, and sometimes just every sentence. Don't go for more than four or five sentences without pausing, because bad things will tend to happen. The frequency of your pauses throughout a speech dictates the rhythm at which the audience will try to follow your words. A good rhythm will enthrall an audience. A poor rhythm will lose an audience's attention because they won't be able to catch up with your words. It's like trying to shoot a basketball through a hoop at that point, except the hoop is constantly moving back and forth, and up and down.

What do I mean by rhythm, and how can I teach it to you? Well, the rhythm of speech is one of those things that is a little difficult to teach and explain, but I can describe to you how to develop your own rhythm.

You can get started on developing your own rhythm by asking yourself this basic question. How would you like to be spoken to if someone were to lecture you on something? Your answer to that question is most likely an excellent foundation from which to establish the way you speak, or your speaking rhythm.

Just think. Do you like it when someone speaks to you with long pauses between sentences, or with short pauses? Do you like it when the rhythm is steady, or erratic? These are things you need to consider and control if you wish to sway an audience's opinion on a particular topic.

One more thing I want to mention is that when speaking, some people are so nervous that their voices waver rapidly as they speak. This is an involuntary physical reaction that should be an indication that public speaking is not for you.

I wish there was a method I could suggest in combating this issue, but I know of no magic cure. If this is a common occurrence with you in your speeches, just be aware that this is one of the few things that the audience will usually interpret as a sign of weakness, and that at the same time, is not really

your fault. It just means that this is a
disadvantage you need to try to
overcome.

80

Chapter 13: Embed Positive Thoughts

And Emotions

How many hours do you normally spend in deliberating and dwelling on the fearful and negative things in your life? Have you spent hours worrying about all the things that could go wrong rather than paying attention and concentrating on what is good, positive and rational? You need to teach yourself how to concentrate your thoughts and emotions so that they can help you move forward towards panic free situations. It is important that you spend a few moments every day in embedding positive thoughts and emotions into your being. You need to train yourself on how to pay attention to things that are both right and rational. Keep in mind that if you continuously focus on the panic, you will never have the confidence to speak publicly.

When you continuously examine and recall your experiences in the past, scrutinising them and "getting in touch with your feelings", you will only strengthen those negative emotions. If you don't want a problem to rule your life, you need to shift your focus away from it. Instead, you should concentrate on what is nice, beautiful, positive, and rational. You will only feel happiness and contentment if you allow yourself to be completely engrossed in the present moment and not living in the past or the future. You can only make your problems worse when you analyse and think about it too much. Today can offer you new opportunities to be a confident speaker if you only allow yourself to live in the present moment.

Do you know why young kids believe that monsters, goblins, and ghosts are real? Most adults believe that these things do not exist in the real world. We know that just because we can imagine the existence of ghosts and monsters does not mean that they do exist. This should be the same treatment you should give your negative thoughts. Just because you can imagine panicking in public, it does not mean that it is real. Continuously thinking about those bad things will only reinforce their fake existence and the other negative feelings that come with them. Always keep in mind that your thoughts are only what you choose to imagine and continuously strengthen in your head. You are what you think you are and if you think you are, you are right.

Have you ever experienced this situation? You are staying alone inside your house and you hear a noise, you get scarred. You are feeling worried and panicky and your head is filled with fearful thoughts. Then suddenly, you hear your phone ring and it's your favourite sister who you have not talked to in months. You suddenly feel attentive and your mood instantly changes. You spend the next hour talking excitedly with your sister. Then, your sister says goodbye, you start feeling worried again and you go back to your fearful mood. Do you know the reason behind this?

It is time you realise that even though you do not realise it, you have more control over your thoughts that you imagine. You can choose to remain in that happy, calm mood after your sister said goodbye by doing everything you can to stop yourself from going back into a fearful state. Through a cognitive-behavioral therapy, your therapist can give you techniques and tools that can help you get over your anxiety and panic and sustain a positive outlook and mindset.

When you decide to change your thoughts, you will see that your emotions will start to feel better. If you decide to act based on rational thoughts even though you are feeling fearful and panicky, you will see that positives emotions and beliefs will soon follow.

You need to accept the truth that there are lot of things in life that are outside your control. But despite that, you need to accept your own life and decide to be strong and brave. You can always decide to be brave whether you are going through difficult times. You should not think that you can only start being brave when you are leaving the house or about to walk on the stage or to start the talk. You should concentrate on learning how you can be brave no matter what situation you are in. You need to learn how to draw on your contentment and inner peace in such a manner that will work best for you. Always remember that you will only achieve fearlessness when you decide to be brave and strong. It is your thoughts that create your emotions. You cannot be panicky when you do not decide to be so. Panic only exists because you think you are going to panic.

Your thoughts about the past linger on things and situations that are not real anymore today. Whatever bad experiences you went through yesterday is done and over with. It is finished and it only has existence inside your mind. You are given a brand new day today which could be better than yesterday. But if you worry about yesterday, you are just ruining your present day. Learning how to focus on today will spell a big difference in your life.

You need to recognise that you are a thought-generating machine. When you do this, you will start slowing down your thoughts so you can let your fears and anxieties die down. Your ANTs or automatic negative thoughts are just that — thoughts. They are not your reality. They do not represent what is true in you and in your life.

We all lean towards thinking too much which could make end up paralysed. That is what they refer to as paralysis by analysis. But whether this is your natural tendency or not, you need to always keep in mind that you have a choice. You can choose whether to be brave or continue to panic. You can choose to focus on your negative thoughts or to look for positive things in your life. The people you see around you don't think about panicking all the time, so it will only happen to them if they allow it, and once you panic once, your mind is very good at replaying it over and over again. You can easily see in a preschool class how were meant to react to fear, where the kids get over excited and move into panic but because they focus on the present moment without thinking too much about the panic afterwards, they allow themselves to move on past the event and continue living with normal levels of fear, which are ultimately there for a

87

very good reason, they just go out of sync sometimes.

Are you suffering from anticipatory anxiety? Well, you have a choice – you can continue thinking about it or you can decide to take the necessary steps and just create other thoughts instead.

Your thoughts are nurtured by your attention. When you give more attention to your negative thoughts, you are actually nurturing them to grow bigger and bigger. When you give more attention to your own progress and to other positive thoughts, you will allow them to become stronger and have "automatic" control over your life.

Chapter 14: Tips And Strategies To Completely Overcome Fear Of Public Speaking

Did you know that professional golfer Tiger Woods grew up with a speech impediment? You may not be able to tell it now, but he grew up stuttering, which made him afraid of speaking in public.

When asked how he overcame this, he said that he focused on fixing his speech impediment. He kept on practicing – even having conversations with his dog – and always kept a positive attitude about things. He also constantly pictured himself in a positive place in order to keep his mindset on the proper path.

We could learn a lot from how Tiger Woods conquered his fear.

First, he identified the root of the problem and concentrated on fixing it before anything else. When he did, he was persistent and never gave up until he got the results he wanted.

Take your time. Do not hurry about things. Remember the phrase "haste makes waste"? Rushing through your speech or your talk will cause more problems. In wanting to get it over and done with as quickly as possible, you may feel the urge to rush through the speech. More often than not, however, fast talking can make breathing more difficult, and the fear is compounded unnecessarily.

According to some experts, there are three key things that you should do when you suddenly find yourself experiencing fear of trying to speak in public:

•Do not show that you are terrified. Keep your face blank or relaxed, control any trembling in your hands and limbs.

•Stand still. Being restless, especially on stage, is a sure sign that you are anxious.

•Do not speak too fast. If you do, you may end up stuttering, thereby worsening the problem. Choose your words carefully and enunciate them. So what if it is very slow? At least they will be comprehensible.

A very good example of the third point is the movie "The King's Speech". In order to overcome a stuttering problem, King George VI was made by his speech therapist to employ pauses when speaking.

Be more proactive. So you joined support groups; should you stop there? Of course not. Expand your social network by taking the initiative in joining more groups and participating in activities that will expose you to more people (you could try a drama class). This will eventually help you become more at ease with the idea of communicating with more than two or three people at one time.

Take classes and training courses. In particular, classes and courses related directly to public speaking will be highly beneficial for anyone looking to fully overcome glossophobia. Not only will these classes help them overcome their fear of public speaking, it will also teach them to be more confident and persuasive when speaking in public.

Joining organizations such as the Toastmasters International is also a good way to reinforce what you have learned in joining classes and training programs. It will get you started in practicing speaking in small, informal groups, until you ease your way to a larger listening audience.

Learn to appreciate the sound of silence. It always helps to relax in a quiet environment. According to ABC anchor Dan Harris, you should try to "stop the chatter". A moment of silence will calm your mind, especially when it is assailed from all sides by various noises and information. This is also an opportunity to focus on what is important and filter all the negative thoughts and chatter which can be a big part of what's holding you back from excelling in public speaking.

For at least 5 minutes each day, try to meditate and allow your mind have a 'workout'. Harris suggests sitting down with your spine straight and supported, say, by the back of a chair. Close your eyes and breathe. Regulate your breathing such that you can feel it go in and out. When your mind wanders, just focus on your breathing. It will bring you back to your focus.

Stock up on knowledge about glossophobia. Fortunately, there is no shortage of self-help materials that will aid you in your fight against this fear. Learn all you can about the condition so you will be in a better position to control and conquer it.

Choose a very good therapist. Pick one that you are comfortable with. If talk therapy is your chosen treatment, choose a therapist that you will have no trouble communicating with. Trust is an important element of any relationship between a patient and a medical professional, so see to it that you trust him or her enough.

Work it out. Did you know that aerobic exercises can also work wonders in helping calm the nerves? Speaking coaches highly recommend getting a substantial amount of exercise on a daily basis, and especially before delivering a speech or talking to a group of people. Even breathing exercises will help a lot, and you can do them practically anywhere, at any time.

Practice, practice, practice. Just like Tiger Woods did. This is especially helpful for those with speech impediments.

Start by delivering speeches covering topics that you consider yourself an expert on or at least knowledgeable on.

Chapter 15: Learn How To Work With A

Crowd

If you have to speak in front of a crowd, whether it is for a meeting, a presentation, or public speaking engagement, you need to learn how to work the crowd—how to be able to speak without stuttering even if a lot of people are looking at you.

There are certain things that you have to do to make this happen, and these are the following:

Learn to Use Space

You can move around the stage. You don't have to dance, but you can walk from one end to the next in order to engage your audience. It would be so awkward if you just stay in place all the time, looking like a stiff tree. You can walk. You can help them understand your thoughts better by making your way to them, or at least, helping them see you as a person and not a talking stick.

Give More of Your Attention to Those Who Nod Their Heads

When speaking in front of a crowd, you'll notice who are listening by checking out who are nodding, and who are actually making sense of what you're talking about. Now, focus on those people so you'd get responses, and so the rest of the audience would feel compelled to butt—or blend—in, and listen to you more intently.

Smize! Go Be Animated

As Tyra Banks would say, Smize! Smile with your eyes. When you do this, it shows that you're sincere with what you're doing instead of just looking bored and stiff, and not knowing what to say. It makes you more alive and realistic—and that's the kind of speaker people want.

Try not to Shift Focus Too Much

When you look from one side of the audience to the other in such a quick manner, people would feel like you're rolling your eyes or that you are extremely nervous. Yes, it's okay to make use of space—but do not try to look from one person to another as if asking for approval. That's not the kind of message you want to impart on your audience.

You Don't Have to Memorize Things

You don't have to prepare and type a long speech and read every single word the way it was written. This would be so monotonous and would just make your audience bored. You can adlib—this is your speech, after all! The more natural it is, the better.

Don't Focus on Your "Mistakes" Too Much

Another cliché: everyone makes mistakes. No one is perfect and no one is immune to errors and the like—but would you actually let those mistakes get you down? No, of course not.

What you should do is just get back up. If you said a wrong word, don't make use of fillers. Try a few seconds of silence, and then make a joke, or just engage the audience.

When you recognize your mistakes, you will easily be able to bounce back from them instead of just feeling like you are a failure. Even the most seasoned public speakers make mistakes. Don't let those errors make you fall off track.

Inject Some Fun into It

Laughter is not only the best medicine, it's also one of the easiest ways to get someone's attention and to keep the atmosphere light and engaging. It's not about making slapstick jokes, but just about showing your wit and being able to make the conversation fun for everyone.

Just because you're making a speech doesn't mean it has to be overly serious, especially when you know that you can inject some humor into it. When laughter pervades in a room, people feel better and they feel like they could reach you, instead of feeling like you're only talking about the things that matter to you. But of course, don't try to make jokes if it's a serious matter (i.e., death, grieving, etc.) Think of your audience.

Your speech should be about everyone—and not just about you.

Chapter 16: Climax

We've already established that I'm one of those freaks who come alive in front of a big audience. The bigger the better as far as I'm concerned. Perhaps it's that yearning for fame thing again. Looking out from the stage into the glare of 700 pairs of eyes, I was in my element.

Basel is a relatively small city home to a handful of large companies. Having worked for two of them in the 16 years I'd spent in the city, I knew many faces in the audience, which spurred me on even more.

The adrenaline kicked in and I felt a satisfying glow as I delivered my speech, "happy birthday" style. I stumbled in a couple of places, but picked up immediately and even managed to play with the crowd in a few places — something that Jane had advised me not to do because it "will isolate the audience that watches it online afterwards". The live audience didn't seem to be bothered by that, as they gave my talk the loudest laughs and applause of the entire event.

I've learned over the years that the single most important thing about making any speech or presentation is to always think about the audience first. In this case, with 700 people each paying 50 Swiss francs to attend the event, they had to come first. If I could excite and move them, surely it would carry over to anybody watching online too.

Unbeknownst to the speakers until the day of the event itself, Harrison had appointed himself Master of Ceremonies. If you've ever experienced a Swiss audience, you'll know that they aren't the most outgoing.

The last production I'd seen at the Musical Theatre was The Rocky Horror Show, famous for its audience members dressing up as the cast and joining in with the action. My husband and I turned out to be virtually the only people dressed in fishnet stockings and suspender belts. Everyone else was in their smart Sunday outfits.

A Swiss audience needs help warming up and Harrison appeared to be doing the opposite. One trainer I work with says: "Some people walk into a room and light it up. Others walk out of a room and light it up".

Despite this – and some of the sessions running way over time, which resulted in a reduced audience for the final session – it seemed to me that people enjoyed the event overall. Being continuously mobbed by "fans" introducing themselves to me, I basked in the glory of being a TEDx star at the drinks reception that followed. My mobile phone was buzzing with messages from friends who had been in the audience or watched the live-streamed event on the internet. As the stage was being dismantled, the organisers, volunteers, and speakers raised a glass together to congratulate each other for a job well done.

Even the discovery, just before I went on stage, that there had been a mistake with my billing in the printed programme (they had printed another speaker's biography in place of mine), could not dampen this moment for me.

Chapter 17: Be Natural

One of the biggest mistakes most people make when giving a public presentation is that they try to impress. Many will use words that sound more sophisticated, giving them an air of intellectualism throughout their speech. Others will try to appear more knowledgeable on the matter than they actually are, creating a false image of being an expert in the field. In the end, such efforts of deception, although well intended, only serve to create additional stress and anxiety. Furthermore, such efforts are usually easy to see through, meaning that most of the audience will recognize the deception at hand. In the end, the best way to reduce stress and anxiety, while also maximizing the value of your presentation, is to be natural. This chapter will reveal four ways in which you can use your natural abilities to bring about the best results possible.

Make it Interactive

You would think that public speaking wouldn't be such a big deal, after all it's nothing more than simply talking to a group of people. Almost everyone has conversations with people on a daily basis, meaning that it shouldn't be an issue. Strangely enough, even those who have a natural gift for carrying on conversations struggle when it comes to public speaking. The main reason for this is that they don't actually use their skills to their advantage. Rather than having a conversation, they try to give a formal presentation, something that is unnatural to their more laid back personality. The trick, therefore, is to make your presentation more interactive, thus turning it into more of a conversation than a formal speech.

Take the time to ask the audience questions. Make sure everyone is following what you are saying so that you know your presentation is having the desired effect. Furthermore, ask interactive questions, such as what people think about a subject, or what they would expect from a scenario you are discussing. In the end, creating an interactive environment takes the stress off of the presenter by making the event more collaborative in nature. This is also a brilliant way to put other minds to work for solving problems or addressing questions that you might not have the answers to. By engaging the audience you can turn any presentation into an informal exchange of thoughts and ideas, making it far more natural as a result.

Take Breaks

Another way that you can be more natural when giving a presentation is to take plenty of breaks. The chances are you don't talk constantly throughout the day, never taking a moment to collect your thoughts or take a drink of water. Why should you act any differently when giving a presentation? If you take a moment to think about what you are going to say when having a conversation do so when giving a presentation. This will help you to keep your thoughts on track, much the same way that you do in day-to-day life. If you try to be superhuman and not take any breaks at all you will only increase the difficulty of the situation, making it harder on yourself than it needs to be.

Additionally, the breaks you take for yourself can actually benefit the audience as well. Just as it is unnatural for a person to talk constantly, so too, it is equally unnatural for a person to constantly listen. In order to process information you need a break in-between the different thoughts being presented. Therefore, pushing through a presentation without taking breaks is not only hard on the presenter, it is hard on those listening as well. However, by taking regular breaks, even just for a sip of water, you not only give yourself the chance to gather your thoughts, you also give the audience the chance to process what you said and prepare for what is next.

Use Your Natural Stance

More often than not a person giving a public presentation will stand the whole time, either behind a podium or just on stage with no other props or furniture of any kind. This often has the result of making the presentation seem even more formal and intimidating. After all, how often do people stand in one place for a lengthy period of time simply talking and presenting information? While some people may feel more comfortable using this format the majority of people don't. Therefore, another way to reduce the stress of the event is to use your natural stance.

If you feel more comfortable sitting when you speak, bring a chair to your event. People may scratch their heads at first, seeing as this isn't the usual way presentations are given. However, the fact is that the audience is sitting, so why shouldn't you? Many people feel self-conscious in a situation where one person is standing while the other is sitting, therefore you might actually help calm people in the audience who would feel uncomfortable if you stood. Alternatively, you may choose to walk around a lot, or you might prefer to stand behind a podium where you can review your notes more freely. In any case, the important thing is to be as comfortable as possible, so always use your natural stance when giving a presentation.

Use Your Natural Voice

Finally, there is the aspect of using your natural voice. Just as using your natural stance can significantly reduce stress and anxiety by making you more physically comfortable, using your natural voice can do the same by making you more mentally comfortable. Again, when you try to use words that aren't a part of your normal vocabulary you only serve to create added stress and anxiety on yourself. The best public speakers are those who are true to themselves. Furthermore, the more natural a person is, the more believable they are. Therefore, using your natural voice will have far greater results than if you alter your voice in an attempt to impress your audience.

Using your natural voice is more than just about the words you use; it also covers the speed in which you speak, as well as your tone and volume. The best speakers are those who virtually converse with their audience. This is because it is easier and more natural to listen to a conversation than a speech. Therefore, if a speech is given as a conversation the audience will receive it better. Again, this is how doing the right thing can benefit both you and your audience, making it a win/win situation. The trick is to always be true to yourself. Not only will this make the job of public speaking easier, but it will also gain the trust and respect of your audience far more than any false pretenses ever will. By being true to yourself you will greatly improve your performance, and thus achieve the success you truly deserve!

Chapter 18: The Art Of Persuasion

Persuasive speeches attempt to change or solidify the beliefs or the attitudes of audience members. Allow me to illustrate:

Several years ago, I was a clinician at a prison in the United States that housed and treated incarcerated sex offenders. It was a fascinating time for me in my professional career, and one of the things that made my job at the prison so interesting was the often-adversarial relationship between clinical staff and custodial staff. As clinicians, we were charged with administering sex offender therapy to some of the most heinous criminals in the state prison system, which meant that most of us felt that at least a portion of them could be successfully rehabilitated. This view of the population at the prison was in direct conflict with many of the prison officers there, most of whom believed that the clinical staff was wasting their time because it was impossible to rehabilitate sex offenders.

Considering this philosophical conflict among the two staff components, the prison leadership decided that it would be a good idea to have a clinician conduct trainings for correctional officers during which the treatment program would be explained. These proposed trainings would have two objectives: the first would be to increase officers' understanding of the sex offender treatment program, and the second would be to persuade them to at least consider that the program was useful to at least some members of the population and thus credible.

I was asked to conduct these trainings every Friday for staff and they were to continue until all the correctional officers had sat through the training. As I prepared for my initial training, I had my two objectives in mind and decided to split the training session into two parts.

The objective for the first part of my training focused exclusively on providing information regarding the contracted agency that provided the sex offender treatment, as well as elements of the treatment program. In other words, in the first part of my training, I addressed the who, what, when, where, and why of the treatment program, keeping it strictly informational.

During the second part of the training, which occurred after a fifteen-minute break, I talked about why we as clinicians thought that the program had value. I cited the clinical rationale that although sex offender treatment may not be effective for every perpetrator, the program was designed to offer interventive tools for those offenders who chose to use them. Given that one of the objectives of the persuasive part of my presentation was to reduce negative stereotypes about the population with whom we all worked, I also discussed the clinical objective to view perpetrators as individuals and to treat them as such, as opposed to simply grouping all men who have committed sex offenses together and making general judgements about them based upon their membership in that group.

I certainly learned a lot about public speaking as I conducted those weekly trainings. One of the most important lessons I learned is that the better prepared I was, the better my training went. I was not as prepared for my first training with those correctional officers as I was for subsequent sessions, and my performance in that first training suffered as a result. Although I had prepared well for the informational part of my presentation, I had not done as great of a job on the persuasive component. To be specific, I had neglected to plan in detail what reasons I was going to give to establish credibility for the program. "Winging it" was not sufficient. In addition, while I had clearly stated the thesis statement of my argument, which was that the sex offender treatment program had potential to change people's lives for the better, I fell short in my quest to support my thesis with hard evidence. I had also failed to anticipate what sort of questions might have been asked by the correctional officers during and after my presentation.

Had I read the following information that details how to prepare a persuasive speech, I would have done a better job that first day.

Setting Up a Persuasive Speech

Here are some questions you must answer in order to prepare and present a persuasive argument that is organized and credible:

•What Will I Talk About? - One of the first tasks of a persuasive speaker is to choose a topic for his presentation. Sometimes the topic will already be chosen because the audience is gathered to discuss or hear about just one topic. For example, a community activist who is trying to gain community support of a citizen neighborhood watch program is already aware that his mission at the next town council meeting is to explain the reasons why such a program would benefit the community.

Speakers who are charged with presenting a topic for a specific course or a speakers' club, such as Toastmasters, often have the option of choosing topics for their presentations. If the topic is your choice, choose a topic that sparks your passion and your interest. It's much easier to research a topic you care about than one that holds no interest for you.

If you have the option of choosing a topic, gain a sense of the occasion of the event. Learn about the factors that are bringing the audience members together. Learning as much as you can about your audience before you choose a topic will make you better able to choose something that interests them.

Once you have established a fair idea of your audience profile, choose a topic that fits the audience and fits the occasion. It would probably be inappropriate, for example, if you were to decide to talk to a group of twenty-something women employed in the food service industry about why men over the age of fifty should exercise regularly. A more appropriate topic for young women working in food service could address the reasons why beginning to plan for retirement at a young age can be very beneficial for the future.

•What is My Goal for This Presentation? - What do you wish to accomplish with your persuasive presentation? Is your mission to simply open people's minds about the topic at hand, or are you calling for a massive change in the way the audience is currently thinking or doing things? If your goal is to simply move their mindsets a little bit, then you may want to use a soft approach. However, if your mission is to get the group to rise up and take action, then it's best to hit them with more passion and verve as you speak to them.

•What Sort of People Make Up My Audience? - Where does your audience currently stand on your topic? Are they inclined to agree with you, or are they leaning more toward the other side of the argument? The more you know about where they stand, the better able you will be to prepare yourself and your speech for them. There are generally three types of people that will be in your audience in regards to where they stand on the issue: there will be those who stand in opposition to your side of the issue, those that are neutral either because they are unaware or have not made up their mind regarding the issue, and those who support your perspective regarding the issue. Let's discuss how to handle people from each group.

Your job with those who disagree with your perspective or your solution regarding the topic at hand is to try and find out why they have the perspective they do. Every situation is different, but you can talk to people who know the audience well, such as the people who invited you to speak to the group. Even better, if possible, you could seek out a few of those who oppose you directly and ask them what motivates them to see things the way they do. You may not be able to change everyone in this group to jump on over and join you on your side, but if you present a sound argument, you may succeed in at least opening the minds of a few opponents by giving them more information regarding the issue, or your side of the issue, than they had prior to your presentation.

As a speaker presenting a persuasive speech, your job with those people who have not yet formed an opinion regarding your topic is to get them to buy into your argument. They may be a bit easier to convince than the than those who do not buy into your argument, but you should not ignore them. Often, undecided audience members simply do not have as much information regarding the topic as the people in the other two groups and it that's the case, you must educate them so that they are informed enough to decide either way.

Your goal with the group of people in your audience who already share your perspective regarding the issue you are discussing may be to convince them to act on their passion in order to help the cause. You may not just want your audience to simply listen; you may want them to act toward affecting change regarding your topic. Audience members who are already on your side are your best candidates for action.

Questions you should be able to answer regarding your audience that may help you as you prepare your speech include the age range of the group, the gender breakdown, shared fears or concerns, values, interests, beliefs, and goals, and obstacles to change regarding their perspective on the issue.

•How Will I Build My Argument? - After you learn the occasion of your presentation and learn as much as you can about your audience, decide on a theme for your speech. What message do you wish to convey to those who will be gathered to listen to you? Your speech should focus on just one idea, which you will clearly state in your thesis statement. Everything else you talk about in your speech should be designed to support your thesis statement. Your thesis statement should be stated within the first few minutes of your speech.

Once you decide on a thesis statement for your persuasive speech, you will conduct your research to find facts that support your argument. Then, you will decide on a strategy for presenting your thesis and your evidence. We will discuss various strategies for presenting a persuasive speech later in this chapter.

•What Sort of Examples and Evidence Should I Include? - As you begin to prepare your argument for your persuasive speech, you are going to want to provide examples and build your stories around concepts that the audience members can understand. Using examples that are familiar to your audience will increase the likelihood that they will be able to empathize with your side of the argument.

If you choose examples and stories that have no bearing on listeners' own lives, they are less apt to see the importance of changing their opinion or taking action toward change. For example, a police sergeant addressing a group of rural high school students in northern

Maine about the dangers of heroin would probably lose the attention of many if he focused his talk on how heroin deaths were up 200% over the previous year in New York City. A better strategy for the sergeant would be to share statistics regarding heroin overdoses that were affecting the rural areas of northern New England.

The best evidence is factual; however, it is worth remembering that two parties can look at the same factual evidence and come up with completely different interpretations. In regards to global warming, for example, both sides of the issue stipulate that there have been measurable changes in Earth's climate over the past several years, but one side declares that the changes are naturally occurring, and the other places the blame for the changes on human use of fossil fuels, believing that continued use of coal and oil will eventually deplete the ozone layer and cause our oceans to rise.

Whatever evidence you use, it is advisable that you combine your factual information with an emotional appeal. Invoking emotion strengthens a persuasive speech because emotions motivate people to action.

•What is the Perspective of the Opposing Viewpoint of my Argument? - Take some time during your persuasive speech to explain the opposing perspectives regarding your argument, and be sure to do so respectfully. Your ability to demonstrate your knowledge of opposing points of view will let the audience know that you have thoroughly researched the issue, which will enhance your credibility and your reputation as a fair-minded speaker and thinker. Point out the flaws in the opposing viewpoint so that your audience has an easier time seeing why your perspective is preferable.

Modes of Persuasion

Modes of persuasion, or rhetorical appeals, are strategies persuasive speakers use to appeal to their audience members. There are three of them: ethos, logos, and pathos.

Ethos refers to the speaker's attempt to use his reputation, or credibility, as tools to persuade his audience. Speakers who are well-known to their audience members have an advantage utilizing this strategy provided their reputation with the audience is positive. For a speaker to establish a strong ethos, he needs to communicate that he is well versed on the topic about which he is speaking. The speaker does this often by presenting both sides of the argument and then stating why his favored perspective is preferable. Secondly, a speaker using ethos will make sure he has a very good understanding of his audience so that he may tailor his speech to gain maximum effectiveness. Finally, those speakers utilizing the ethos strategy will cite evidence that is deemed to be credible by audience members or by the public at large.

The second mode of persuasion employed by persuasive speakers is logos. The logos strategy uses logical arguments and valid reasoning to appeal to the intellectuality of the audience. Logical appeals use facts from widely respected sources to build foundations for arguments. In addition, they use valid and sound argument strategies, such as deductive reasoning and conditional statements, to shape their arguments in a way that appear to be logical to listeners. The logos strategy is especially strong because it is difficult to argue against sound reasoning, particularly if that reasoning is backed up by information that is deemed factual by listeners.

Pathos is the third method of persuasion and it focuses on appealing to the emotions of the listeners. The goal of the persuasive speaker using the pathos strategy is to exploit the strong emotional connection the audience members have with the subject matter. Several years ago, I attended a presentation by a chapter of Mothers Against Drunk Driving (M.A.D.D.) during which graphic photos of automobile accidents caused by drunk drivers were shown to audience members. Those photos served to evoke strong reactions in the audience, as did stories told by survivors and loved ones of people who had died because of the actions of intoxicated drivers. Photos and storytelling are effective tools utilized by speakers employing the pathos strategy of persuasive speech.

A subtler way of using the pathos strategy is to establish a personal connection with audience members. It is a well-known fact that people are more apt to accept what you are telling them if they like you. If you can demonstrate some common bond between you and the audience, you may be well on your way to getting your message across with the help of the pathos strategy.

Using Deductive Reasoning in Your Argument

Persuasive speakers use deductive reasoning in their arguments when they make general statements, or premises, that are assumed to be true and then draw a conclusion about a more specific situation or event. Consider this example:

•Premise: "All police personnel in Springfield have graduated from college."

•Premise: "Justin and Tracy are both police officers in Springfield."

•Conclusion: "Therefore, Justin and Tracy have college degrees."

The conclusions that are reached through deductive reasoning are always going to be true if the premises are true. If the premises are false, however, the argument may still be valid even though the conclusion may be false. Take a look at this example:

- Premise: "All politicians are dishonest."
- Premise: "Dominic is a politician."
- Conclusion: "Therefore, Dominic is dishonest."

If we view this example logically, it is a valid argument that uses deductive reasoning. However, though the argument is valid, the conclusion may be untrue (it is highly doubtful that every single politician is dishonest).

Using Inductive Reasoning in Your Argument

Another way to structure arguments is by using inductive reasoning, which is the opposite of deductive reasoning. Inductive reasoning statements uses specific situations and then makes general assumptions about larger groups based upon those situations. Here's an example of an argument using inductive reasoning:

- Premise: "Katrina sells insurance.
- Premise: "Katrina is a very hard-working woman.

•Conclusion: "Therefore, all insurance salespersons work hard."

Here's another example:

•Premise: "I prepared and organized this presentation to the best of my ability."

•Premise: "This presentation went very well and I was well-received."

•Conclusion: "I need to spend quality time preparing and organizing all of my presentations."

Scientists use inductive reasoning to construct theories about how two or more variables react to changes in each other. Note, however, that even though the premises in an inductive argument may both be true, it does not always mean that the conclusion will be true. This point is illustrated in the first inductive reasoning example above.

Choose a Structure for your Persuasive Speech

There are three different structural strategies that are commonly used in persuasive speaking:

1.The Problem-Cause-Solution Strategy – This strategy can be very effective when used correctly. The speaker spends the first part of the speech outlining the nature and the causes of the problem including history, severity, and why it is a problem in the first place. The speaker may include statistics or other evidence that the issue is, in fact, a problem. In addition, the speaker may want to tell a story or cite anecdotal evidence designed to appeal to the emotional side of the listeners.

The second part of a speech using this strategy focuses on the solution posed by the presenter. The mission is to explain the solution so that the audience understands how and why it will solve the problem. Speakers using the problem/solution structure should spend time thinking about questions the audience may have regarding the problem and the solution so that they can plan responses.

An example of a persuasive speaker using the problem-cause-solution structure would be the argument President-elect Donald J. Trump used throughout the presidential campaign in 2016. As he traveled around the country campaigning, he spent much time discussing the "problem" of illegal immigration and offered the idea of building a wall along the border between Mexico and the United States as his "solution."

2.The Comparison Strategy – The comparison format is best used when comparing two or more items side-by-side so that the speaker can point out and demonstrate the superiority of one item over the others. The speaker accomplishes this by focusing on specific qualities or features that make the preferred item appear to be the better choice. Salespeople use this technique all of the time as they try to get customers to prefer their products over similar items.

3.Monroe's Motivated Sequence - Monroe's Motivated Sequence is a method for designing persuasive speeches, developed in the mid-1930s by Alan H. Monroe, who was a professor at Purdue University. Monroe's method relies on logic and psychology to motivate audiences to action, not just open their minds to an alternate viewpoint. Monroe's Motivated Sequence contains five steps. As I discuss each one below, I illustrate how the step works using the same example:

•Step One – Gain Your Audience's Attention - Monroe was a big believer in grabbing the audience's eyes, ears, and minds from the moment you begin your speech. He was concerned that, all too often, people fail to do this by neglecting to make eye contact, or by reading their speech from pages they hold in front of them. Speakers who can get their listeners to sit up and take notice have a much better chance of holding their attention throughout the presentation. Gaining audience attention can be accomplished by making a shocking statement or quoting a startling fact, telling a powerful story using comedic or dramatic effect, posing a question, or showing a moving visual. Whatever attention-grabbing technique you use, make sure that it is designed to strike the senses of your audience in a way that will move them.

Example: Several years ago, I was teaching courses for college credit aboard Coast Guard ships and, prior to each patrol, I would board the ship to discuss the educational program with Coast Guard personnel and try to get as many to sign up as I could. I was nervous the first time I had one of those meetings, but I was organized and prepared and I had a good idea of the needs of my audience. In order to draw them into the idea of taking a course or two as they were at sea working on a ship, I asked them to imagine earning college credit while working aboard their ship in the middle of the ocean! I then talked about the uniqueness of the program and how it was the only one like it in New England. I also talked about the power of education and how gaining a college could not only help them in the Coast Guard, but also for the rest of their lives.

•Step Two – Establish the Need for Change - During this step of Professor Monroe's method, the speaker's goal is to convey the seriousness of the topic being discussed and let the audience know that something must be done to solve the problem that is being presented to them. The speaker accomplishes this goal by offering facts and opinions from reputable sources, testimony, stories, and examples, all of which are directly relatable to the listeners' values and interests. By the end of this part of the persuasive speech, audience members should be eagerly listening and waiting to hear the rest of what you are presenting to them, or your solution to whatever problem you have put in front of them.

Example: During my initial meeting with Coast Guard personnel assigned to those cutters, I talked about the difficulty of taking college courses while one was assigned to a ship, given that most Coast Guard ships were only in port for two months and then out for two months. I also talked about the "down time" Coast Guard personnel experienced while at sea and how taking a college course could fill that void.   Finally, I talked about the challenges they faced if they left the Coast Guard and tried to seek work without a college degree in the private sector. I hoped that I had defined the need for change as I spoke.

•Step Three – Satisfy the Need - In this step, the speaker offers the solution to the issue he or she has discussed in the previous step. It is not enough to simply let them know what the proposed solution is; it is also critical to share with them how the solution will help solve the problem. Explain your solution to the issue clearly and concisely so that audience members can picture how it will work in their minds. Illustrate your solution with examples and cite evidence of its effectiveness, such as pilot programs or feasibility studies, if you have them.

Example: To satisfy the Coast Guard employees' need for education, I took the time to explain how the program worked. We reviewed what courses would be offered, the schedule and required workload for each course, and contingency plans in case class sessions had to be cancelled in the event of Coast Guard operations. This part of my presentation got easier after I had gone out several times to teach, as I could provide them with real-life success stories to illustrate how the program worked for students who had gone before them.

• Step Four – Ask Your Audience to Visualize the Possibilities - This step requires the speaker to appeal to the emotional side of listeners, whereas the previous steps largely focused on appealing to their logic. The goal is to direct listeners to imagine the potential outcomes of the proposed solution, as well as what could happen if no action is taken or if an alternative solution is put into place.

Example: This is the fun part of using Monroe's Motivated Sequence. I asked my future students on those ships to imagine themselves being able to take courses at their place of employment, AND have it paid for in full by their employer! I also asked them to imagine how great it would be to earn an Associate's or a Bachelor's degree in part due to successfully completing courses while at sea. Plenty of them were able to visualize their success.

• Step Five – Ask Your Audience to Act - The final step in the Motivated

Sequence is for the speaker to propel audience members into action to address the issue that has been discussed. Speakers who use Monroe's Motivated Sequence realize the importance of directly asking listeners for their participation, and making it as easy as possible to participate right when the presentation ends. You should know exactly what sort of action you want them to take and prepare accordingly. The speaker needs to have whatever they may need in order to act, including phone numbers, application forms, petitions, pens, pencils, maps to specific locations, or credit card processors. The more that you can facilitate action, the less likely they will fail to act.

Example: I made sure I had everything those men and women needed to sign up for courses immediately following my talks. I had college registration forms, course sign-up forms, pens, calendars, college brochures, and I even arranged for the ship's educational services officer to be present to answer any questions prospective students had regarding financial aid. If anyone wanted to sign up for a course that day, which is what I encouraged them to do, I made it very easy for them to do so.

To summarize, persuasive speaking can be great fun if you take the time to do it right. Like any other presentation, though, the amount of time, energy, and creativity you put into it is directly related to what you will get out of it. People who are able to influence the opinions of others and persuade them to act on those opinions are true leaders.

Questions to Ponder:

1.If you are already a persuasive speaker, what mode of persuasion have you used in the past: ethos, logos, pathos, or some combination of the three? Is it useful to consider using other mode or mode combinations? If you have never given a persuasive presentation before, which mode appeals to you and why?

2.How can you improve your oral communication skills to be a powerful persuasive speaker? What is your plan for doing so?

Chapter 19: Is There Any Connection

Between

English and public speaking?

SSo many times I have seen people, they hesitate to come on the stage just because they are not good in English. Is there any relationship between English and public speaking? I doubt, just because if someone is good in English that doesn't mean that that person will be good on the stage, not necessarily.

And just because if someone is not good in English, even that doesn't mean that person can't be good on the stage. English and public speaking, these are two different skills. I remember joining English speaking classes at the age of 30.I failed in ninth standard and if you fail in 8th or 9th , that shows how focused you were in your studies .

But unfortunately you learn languages in these years, we don't learn languages in graduation and I don't even remember the face of my English teacher, but when I came to Mumbai in the corporate world, my boss told me, "Praveen if you want to survive here you have to improve your English" and I joined English speaking classes, basic English speaking classes.

And in that class, I used to learn English sitting besides 12-

13-year-old kids. But that doesn't mean that after that class or after improving my English I became good on the stage or good in my presentation,

No, not at all. I used to struggle in front of people, I started learning public speaking skills a few years ago and now that is helping me to present myself effectively in front of people, but English and public speaking are two different skills.It needs different learning, different ways of practicing.

So it doesn't matter in which language you speak, if you want to improve your public speaking skills, you have to learn

public speaking the way you learn English or the way
you learn Singing, the way you learn dancing, because even public speaking skill is a learnable skill.

14. How to motivate your audience?

Sometimes people ask this question to me, "Praveen, how to motivate the audience? Or how to make the audience laugh from the stage? Many times people ask this question to me that, "Praveen, how I can go on the stage and start sharing stories with the people, so they just listen to me? The answer to all these questions is very simple, start doing this in your personal life.

You can't motivate the audience if you are not motivating the people in your life, like your family, your friends, your colleagues.

You can't make the audience laugh, if you're not making your family and friends laugh in your personal or professional life. You can't share stories from the stage if you are not sharing stories in your personal life with your families and friends or maybe sometimes with strangers

When you start doing all this in your personal life, it is a little easy to do this on the stage, but why we should do this? The answer is because your stage personality should not be different from what you are in your personal life.

What you are in reality, your stage personality should be a hundred percent true reflection of what you are in your personal or professional life.

So next time if you want to make people laugh or if want to motivate people or inspire people or want to share stories start doing this in your personal life on a regular basis.

15. Is public speaking skill evolving?

Every skill is evolving in this world. Let's consider singing, the kind of music, the kind of songs we used to listen to few years ago, are we listening the same kind of music or songs now? No. Singing has evolved. Take dance, the kind of dance we used to watch a few years ago, are we watching the same kind of dance now? No.

The dancing has evolved; even public speaking is a skill.

Has public speaking evolved or is public speaking evolving? Yes, The first time I realized it, when I watched the video named, "I see something" from Dananjaya Hettiarachchi. He's a world champion of public speaking. Even before "I see something" I had seen lots of motivational videos, a lot of talks, but every time I used to see that, I used to feel , " Wow the speaker is good, fantastic but speaker is not like me, he's special, he's different but when I saw "I see something" by Dananjaya Hettiarachchi, I felt for a moment that , "wow ! he is just like me" I think this is the evolution of public speaking that even if you are standing in front of 10,000 people, the person who is watching you should feel that you are just like him, you are speaking to him, speaking for him.

This is the way public speaking has evolved now. Not only Dananjaya Hettiarachchi even Mohammed Qahtani, Daren Tay and all these are the world champion of public speaking when you watch their videos you feel that "oh my God, this is just like my story, he's not different, he's speaking to me."

So next time when you are going on the stage try to speak as if you're speaking to your friend at a tea stall. But that is difficult, not easy but try to speak like that, because when you speak like that, when the audience feels that you are just like them. It is very easy to connect.

Chapter 20: The Two Main Ingredients

Of The Art Of Public Speaking

A. Reading

Whether you are at the library, at your office, whether it is in your home or elsewhere, reading a good book has undeniably, very beneficial advantages. You can condition your mind or change your mindset through reading.

In order to become an accomplished public speaker, you need to nurture your culture of reading. All those motivational speakers presenters etc are all big readers. Reading a book whether it falls under novels, fiction or under any other useful book categories has tremendous advantages as far as public speaking is concerned. Not only it broadens your imagination, enriches your vocabulary but shapes up your personality among many other advantages. When reading, do not hesitate to make use of the dictionary and also take note of new words, expressions that catch your attention. You can never learn to become a great public speaker and despise reading.

B. Your memory

Your good memory during a presentation, for instance, is of an utmost importance when it comes to remembering names, dates, sequences of past events, names of people you have just met etc. That is one the tools that will excitingly impress your audience. Now if you think your memory is not good enough, there are many audiovisual materials out there that will be able to help you in that regard. But in addition to that, I'm going to share with you some of my favourite techniques that I have used to improve my memory as well as the food that is highly recommended for memory boost. They are absolutely Amazing and do work.

The power of association: this a simple technique which consists of associating a name or something you would like to remember with an image; for example, if you want to remember Mrs Closette's name, all you need to do is to associate her name with the picture or image of your closet, and you will not forget her name the next time you see her.

Another method: is to use the power of your subconsciousness. This is is very helpful especially when it comes to learning a foreign language. What you do is to let that tape or CD player run the whole night but the volume is kept very soft, enough for you to sleep but being in a space where it almost feels like you were semi-awake. I have used that method too and it worked fantastically well for me!

You can also improve your memory by reading aloud and repeating what you want to retain or recall. Do not read without thinking. Be critical, see whether you have any objection to what you are reading. keep your reading live and interesting; that way your memory will serve you right!

Breathing method: Just like your yoga coach will teach you, is very helpful too. You can do your breathing exercises in the morning for instance. Open your windows wide and breath in and out repeatedly for few minutes every day.

Food to improve one's memory includes avo, coconut oil, beans, legumes, blueberries, broccoli, dark chocolate, red cabbage, Rosemary, spinach, sunflower seed, tomato, whole grain.

Self-confidence a must

Believing in yourself is one of the virtues every ambitious person or any person willing to succeed in life should strive for. That is the same drive that works you up very early in the morning to sit in your study and prepare for your next meeting. You cannot fake it, because your audience will soon read it right through you, from the first words you say. Which means you 've got to make a conscious effort to believe in yourself. Tell yourself every day " I can do this"

Now as a public speaker, it is crucial that you should feel comfortable and in charge of your audience, you should not let your audience intimidate you or disturb your serenity. Instead feel free, relaxed, and confident. Do not be afraid to display your great personality. In order to do all that, you will need to do is immerse yourself in the subject or topic you are going to speak about very passionately.

How to overcome timidity

Timidity could just be your worst enemy as a public speaker. Unless you conquer that paralysing emotion, public speaking can be a nightmare.

Timidity, as much it is a natural human emotion, can be a serious handicap to those who wish to become great public orators, and can also make you ran away from wonderful opportunities of success in life, because one was not able to express his or her ideas adequately at the right time, given a chance. And I know how it feels, judging from my own personal experience, that is why I'm able to give you the best possible advice that personally helped me overcome that derailing emotion. I remember as a young man, I had to attend a youth camp that was organized by the Church. And as usual, they had sessions of debates and discussions about common issues of life and their impact on the youth. It was my first time to be part of such a venture and I never knew that the leader made sure that each and everyone had his or her fifteen " minutes of fame" by saying something! Now you can imagine how anxious I became as my turn rapidly approached! That time, all I wished was to grow wings and fly through the window. But it literally felt as though I was growing feathers on my skin! All of the sudden, you run of ideas, your throat gets dry and swells a little, your legs start to shake, you start to sweat and you don't know what to do with your hands. It really sounds very bad, doesn't it? Guess what?learning from that awful experience, it took me just over three months to be on top of my game! As I applied these techniques that I am revealing to you. later on in life, I became a life coach and a public speaker throughout central Africa and abroad. So everybody is able to overcome timidity, it is an emotion that one can master once one realises that it is a natural and normal emotion and that one is able to use it positively. Those are the two fundamental principles you need to remember. No need to staff your system with medications that will soon or later make you pay the fatal price. Do not let any feeling of anxiety   stop you when you are to speak in public, always remember, that that particular emotion is normal and it actually exudes your desire to give your best. Even the greatest orators of all time, still experience those moments, but how you deal with them is what makes the difference. When one is about to speak or take action, the whole body is alerted, the muscles tense, the heartbeat enhances, you start breathing faster. All this mobilisation of the body is caused by the adrenal gland called adrenaline. The efflux of that substance is produced spontaneously when we stand to speak or take action with at the watchful eye of an audience. If the situation is habitual, like speaking to your mum, for instance, that emotion stays moderated and would not cause any anxiety. But whether the situation is usual or unusual, always remember that the moment that precedes the action is the most challenging. As soon as you start speaking the tension fades away, because the excess energy accumulated has finally found an exit. From your first pronounced words, the momentum starts to build quite nicely. Never try to think of that feeling rather focus on being confident the all time, because if you display an attitude of someone who is confident, your audience, ultimately, will have confidence in you. They will carefully listen to what you will have to say. That trust and confidence you earn from your audience will give you some assurance you never thought possible. So in order not to be overwhelmed by the feeling, find something else to do and get busy even at the last minute. Remember your anxiety is caused by hormonal discharges that prepare for action. So please make sure not to be inactive. And still, in a bid to overcome that issue of timidity, train yourself to speak in front of a mirror. I know it may sound crazy but it works. Then train yourself by speaking gradually, first with a sibling or a parent then in front of two or three friends or even more. And always remember or tell yourself that your audience is actually not hostile and is waiting to receive with meekness what you are about to say; that each and every individual of the audience has his or her own worries. So go ahead and deliver your speech. You can also train yourself at your workplace with your colleagues. Find a topic you are very passionate about, while on your lunch break, engage the whole group and do that more often and you will be amazed how this will start to flow so naturally.

Chapter 21: Have Your Tools

Speaker's Sheet

Your speaker's sheet is going to be essential if you plan to get outbound speaking gigs. You don't necessarily need one for when you do your own events, but it's still a great idea. Know that more than likely, you will eventually be asked to speak for outbound gigs if you are getting yourself out there. This is a great thing. In fact, this should be a goal!

Usually to get paid to speak, you're not hired by one person with one phone call, like you might be with coaching or consulting. The way the meeting planning business works is the meeting planner spends a lot of time going through speaker materials. Then they get on the phone with a few speakers to see whose personality they like and feel like they click with.

After that, they take your materials to a meeting with a committee or another decision-maker, who you almost NEVER have access to.

That means your marketing materials HAVE to tell your story. Speak volumes. And, make you look like a pro.

Your speaker's sheet is like a resume version of you as a speaker. There are key elements that you want to make sure are in place so that you can secure a job.

Your speaker's sheet, in effect, will answer these seven questions that decision-makers would ask you in person at a first meeting:

1. How would you describe your area of expertise?

2. Whom do you work with and give presentations to?

3. What are the benefits of hiring you—
for the leaders of the organization?
for the participants in the ranks?
for organizational progress?

4.What have you done that makes you an expert?

5.Which groups have you worked with before?

6.What did participants think of your contribution?

7.How can you be reached for more information?

There are seven corresponding "must-have" elements that you want to make sure are covered in your speaker's sheet:

1. Topics/Programs

2. Target Audience

3. Benefits (especially in headlines)

4.Biography

5. Client List

6. Testimonials

7. Contact (Booking) Information

Now, even if you have all of these elements in place, what turns it into a stronger "must-have" piece that represents you? In a word: Personality. Use bold, creative, unique graphics and action photos that support your brand

and set you apart from your competition. Follow up with a strong logo and a powerful tag line. This is all part of your visual brand.

Video Reel

The next most important tool a professional keynote speaker has is a strong video reel. Ideally, you should have an updated "demo reel" every year, incorporating recent successes along the way. Always strive to get video footage of your events. That footage is worth gold!

Use more than one camera angle because that adds perspective and depth to the final video. Try to get audience reactions, like laughter, in the audio track. When corporate event planners hire keynote speakers, they are buying buzz. They're buying audience interaction, both during your speech and afterward. If they see that in your video, it will increase your chances for success.

Now keep in mind that in order to have this footage you will always want to be recording. I have used recordings from all kinds of devices, from phones to professional cameras. Whenever you speak, do your best to get some footage if you can. I myself started off with an inexpensive camera that I could use to record every time I spoke. I also started off just using my phone, but as I have grown in my career, I have been able to purchase better equipment.

If I can't get someone to stand behind the camera, I simply make sure to record with a wide angle that will have me displayed the entire time. I will purposely find ways to take short breaks so that I can change the angel of the camera.

When it comes to your video reel, I do not recommend doing it yourself if you don't have professional experience with editing. You can go to an outsourcing site to get someone else to take your footage and put together a great video reel. Keep in mind that your reel is a highlight video, so it doesn't need to be extremely long. I would say anything longer than three minutes is a bit too much. When you think about commercials, they are only 30 seconds. When someone starts your video, you have less than nine seconds to grab their attention, and for a promotion video it's going to be only a few minutes that you will be able to keep their attention. So when doing your video, keep that in mind.

I have included some incredible examples of video reels on my website, bonus.publispeakingsuccess.com

Website

Your website is going to be your base. I've got to be honest. These days, if you do not have yourself highlighted on your very own website, you are not going to be taken seriously. Please don't throw up just any kind of site. I recommend never using one of those sites that display the name of the company at the bottom, as it shows that you didn't pay for the site to be live. These are typically the sites where you were able to host your website for free. Invest in your site so that you can have something customized. I personally prefer to have a Word Press website, or I will use software that allows me to simply drag and drop and create capture pages. I have a resources tab for this on my website, bonus.SpeakingForProfits.com.

There are a few ways you can get your website done. You can do it yourself. This will take you some time to be able to do, especially if you have no experience with designing websites.

I see a lot of people try to do their website on their own that are not experienced in this. This results in a low success rate. You don't want to cut corners on your website.

You could then hire someone on an outsourcing website for pennies on the dollar. In this case, you would still want

165

to have some knowledge of web design. You need to know the content that you want on your website. These are things you will have to send to the designer. You need to know the colors of your site. How you want it to look. I typically will find another site that I like and use it as a guide. You need to know how many pages and what pages.

I normally recommend this way to my S.Y.S.T.E.M. Mastery students. While I teach them how to design a website from scratch, I don't think that you should do that if you don't have to. But at least know how to do so, so that you are able to do the updates to your website.

Here are a few items that I believe your website should have, especially for those who are looking to get booked as speakers.

• A brief biography / speaker profile
• Media coverage that you've had to date

- Information about the 2-5 keynote speeches you offer; make sure they sound compelling
- A list of recent speaking gigs (paid or unpaid)
- A link to your showcase video
- A couple of well-phrased client testimonials
- Your speaker headshot (ideally professionally photographed)
- Details about any publications, awards, professional bodies, or other impressive info

Business Card

On my business card that I use primarily for booking speaking gigs, I have a cover of my book on one side and on the other I have that I am a speaker and educator. I make sure to not have a whole lot of other things on my business card outside of that. This is so important to keep in mind when it comes to your business card. The reason is because the point of this particular card is to get hired as a

167

speaker, not for everything else. If you have too much going on, you will confuse the person. A confused mind does nothing.

The reason you should have a copy of your book on one side is because you really want your business card to stand out. We get so many cards that many times they all will go into a box and be forgotten. However, when you create one that will stand out, it will help you to stay out of those boxes more often.

A Book

Before I get to talking about having a book, I don't want you to allow the fact that you don't have a book deter you or delay you from getting out there and delivering your talks. Don't let that be an excuse not to get started.

In fact, I teach on how to have a book written in 30 days or less. I've actually been able to show my students how to have their book done in a weekend, so I know that you can absolutely get your book done. There are a few reasons why you want to have a book as a speaker. One reason is because it's a sure way to get booked as a speaker. A book is the best business card and/or speaker's sheet that you could give to a decision maker. I set a goal to mail out four books to decision makers per month. You would not believe how many doors this has opened for me.

The next reason you want to have a book is because when you are delivering your talk, you want to be able to give someone else additional value.

When you do a great job with your talk, 100% of the time, people will want to buy from you. I love selling books because they are tools that people will never ever throw away, they will redirect my readers to connect further with me, and they make me the certified expert.

I recommend that if you are doing any kind of talk, that you have a book. Your book doesn't have to be extremely long, either. Look at this book you are reading right now. Just good enough to give some additional value, to increase your value.

Another reason you want a book is because in some situations, the decision maker may not necessarily be able to pay you to speak. What they can do is buy your books in bulk. To me, this is always a great alternative, especially if it is going to get you in front of a substantial audience. The event host can make sure that everyone gets a copy of your book as well. This is again a strong way to increase your value.

I want to add a little story to this as well, of two incredible speakers that I saw at an event. There was first a young lady who got up at this amazing conference to tell her story and talk about branding. She had an amazing presentation. Her website was incredible. However, when she was done she wasn't really giving anything else of value. I could tell that many of the attendees wanted more information, because as she finished they all lined up to come and speak to her.

Then the next speaker came up. He was extremely late starting, but his talk was also amazing! He was so great that we quickly forgot all about the fact that he was late. At the end of his talk he told everyone to come and meet him in this room so they could get an autographed copy of his book. I promise you when I say this, about 80% of the room came over to buy his books. He sold out!

I remember watching the woman who had spoken before him in complete amazement, because she was watching the same audience who just got in line to tell her how great she was go and buy not one but up to three books on average at a time.

Visionary Speakers! If you don't have one, get your books done today! If you would like to know more about my book writing programs, go to www.Abookin30days.com.

Chapter 22: Feedback

(WHETHER YOU WANT IT OR NOT)

Everyone's a critic. People will want to give you feedback. This is most likely the hardest part of the toast, speech, workshop, or presentation. It was tough enough just getting up there, being vulnerable, keeping it together, and finishing. And now, comes the toughest part.

What's interesting about this is that 99 people can say you were wonderful and one person will say you were so-so. Most of us dwell on the one person. For some reason, we allow them to validate the fears we had all along.

Earlier I shared with you the very first seminar I had done as a Professional Speaker. At the end of that first week, I was doing a seminar in Terra Haute, Indiana. It was a small group of about 40 people. Sitting in the front row, right in the middle, was a gentleman who clearly was not in the mood to be entertained. My style is one where I prefer people to learn and enjoy their day at the same time. But it's really up to them how they want their side of the experience to progress. I know that now. I didn't realize it that day.

The rest of the audience seemed to be enjoying themselves and we worked through the first portion of the morning. The seminar started at 9:00 and our first break was at 10:30. He walked up to me and asked if he could speak with me for a moment. I said, "of course." He then said, "Why don't you knock off trying your jokes out on us and just give us the information we came to learn? I'm a trainer for _____(very large international company) and was also a trainer while serving in the United States Air Force. If you want to be a stand-up comedian, go to a nightclub where you can do that."

Needless to say, I was floored. He had taken all the wind out of my sails. I realize now that I let him take the wind out of my sails. Eleanor Roosevelt said that no one can make you feel inferior without your consent. I gave that man permission to change my entire approach.

I was much shaken during the next segment of the seminar, which ran from 10:45 to 11:45. We broke for lunch and I called the Faculty Director and told her what the man had said to me. Her response was clear and very supportive. "That man came in with his expectation of the day. He trains at _____ and trained in the United States Air Force. That's a very different style than we expect from you. We contracted with you because this is what the majority of adults who attend our seminars expect from their day. You're doing an amazing job. Spend the rest of your day focusing on the people in the room who are truly enjoying the experience and learning great skills from you. And, trust me, they are in that room." She was right. Every once in a while, I would make eye contact with him and he'd just roll his eyes. He did stay the entire day though. That was a plus! The attendees handed in their evaluation forms and, as the Faculty Director said they would, they had a great time and learned very valuable skills.

Anytime you receive feedback that is negative in any way, take a deep breath, look at the contributor, and simply say, "Thank you for your input. I appreciate it." It won't do you any good to argue or try to explain yourself. You don't have to. This is your presentation, not theirs. They showed up ready to be disappointed. So think about this; they met their level of expectation. It was about them; not you. I think you're getting it now!

Most of us remember the negative feedback we get when we put ourselves out there. But if you keep playing that feedback in your mind, eventually you will believe them. That negative feedback is simply somebody else's perception.

A friend of mine, who is a Professional Speaker as well, says that you need to change the recordings in your mind. Simply hit "rewind," "erase," and then record your own positive messages over them.

On the other hand, if you do receive negative input from more than one person, think about the validity of it. Run it by somebody you trust and ask them to give you honest feedback.

Not all feedback is something to slough off and ignore. The areas in my life where I have grown the most are when somebody else brought something to my attention and I was willing to be open to it.

I was delivering an Assertive Communications course in Phoenix, Arizona, one day to an all-women audience of about 95 women. On the first break, one of the ladies came up to me, introduced herself, and told me she was also a Speaker. Other Professional Speakers will tell you that those who want to give you the most feedback are in the same industry.

She said, "I don't know if you realize that you are doing this, but you have called this group of women "guys" at least three times since you started."

I said, "I didn't realize that. What did I say exactly?" I was truly interested in this feedback. I thanked her profusely and did not make that mistake again. I'm grateful to her to this day for bringing that faux pas to my attention.

As I mentioned earlier, you will not be aware of the peculiar speech habits you have unless you hear them in a recording or if somebody else is kind enough to bring them to your attention. Feedback is a valuable tool to help you progress in your skill level. Not everybody wants the audience to fill out an evaluation sheet, but, from my experience, you can't fix what you don't know needs fixing. If you know your audience because you work with them, are in a networking group with them, or are in your community and you know them well, it's probably not necessary to have them fill out an evaluation sheet. But if you're in front of a group of strangers, raw feedback could help you tremendously. Take it for what it is and determine how to move forward with it.

Chapter 23: Giving A Eulogy- How To

Be Thoughtful And Articulate

Being asked to give a eulogy at a funeral is an honor, but can also be a responsibility that brings a lot of anxiety and emotion. It is common to get nervous about speaking in front of others and not knowing what to say on a sad, sensitive, and emotional occasion. Here are things to keep in mind when preparing a eulogy.

Before you start writing the eulogy, try to contact whoever is in charge of the funeral. Ask them what songs will be sung, if the deceased had a favorite Bible verse or saying that will be shared at the funeral. Also ask if anyone else is speaking as well. This information will help you line up your eulogy with a phrase from one of the songs, or you can incorporate the deceased's favorite verse or saying as the opening or closing of your eulogy.

Take some time to reflect on the life of the deceased. What were some great personality traits that they shared throughout their life? What was the legacy that they left behind? Are there any stories that demonstrate these qualities that you could share? Sit down and write down all of the stories that come to mind of you and the person or their family. Also, write down descriptive words that come to mind describing this person.

Look over what you've written down and you will probably begin to see some common themes. Use these to guide your eulogy. A eulogy is especially meaningful when the one giving it makes it unique and specific to the personal qualities that the deceased had. Be sure to focus on the positive qualities that the person offered when they were alive.

Consider also the tone and mood of the funeral. Did the person die tragically young? Was it an elderly person who passed away peacefully? Or was it someone who had been struggling with a long-term illness for quite some time? Take the situation into account as you determine the mood and tone of your speech. If they lived a long and vibrant life, their funeral will be more of a celebration of life. If their life seemed to end too soon, the tone of the funeral will be a greater mourning and struggle.

Write down your eulogy and rehearse it a few times. Saying it out loud will help you realize if a phrase sounds wrong, or maybe that the story you want to share is not appropriate. Don't leave it to the last minute. You want it to be genuine, meaningful, and honoring of the deceased.

It is perfectly acceptable to get emotional while delivering a eulogy. Do not be embarrassed; this is simply part of the grieving process. Everyone at the funeral is there to grieve with you and they will join in your sadness. So, if you start to choke up during the eulogy, take a moment to compose yourself and keep going.

Remember that you are helping to facilitate the process of grieving. As you invest some time to write a thoughtful eulogy, you show respect to the deceased and their family in their time of mourning.

Chapter 24: No Dad Jokes Allowed

I have always been a pretty funny guy. This is reflected in my laid-back style of presenting.

Unlike the Public Speaking Blueprint though, it took me years to be able to effectively teach others the use and how to create humour in their talks. The more I learnt about humour and how to teach it to others. the more I realised how much I was underperforming myself in this area.

Being funny when you present funnily enough doesn't require you to be a funny person day to day. Often many comedians are found to be very dry straight edged people. They have, however found the secret to constructing a humorous talk.

Funny speakers, and particularly standup comedians are great storytellers. Most speakers don't aspire to be standup comedians. They do, however, aspire to share their message as effectively as possible. Humour is your unfair advantage.

I am not talking necessarily about the roll on the floor, quote for decades humour that shows like "The Simpsons" or movies such as "The Hangover" have created; getting your audience to laugh is enough.

Once you get a laugh, herd mentality kicks in. Notice when you watch a comedian's skit or funny movies along on TV, for the most part you don't laugh out loud. Watch the same skits or movies in a group environment, and laughs are aplenty.

This is what we want to create.

If you still aren't sold on the effect of humour check these out. (Credit: Do you talk funny? By David Nihill)

Top Five Funniest Movies of All Time:

Airplane! 3

The Hanover 2.4

The Naked Gun 2.3

Superbad 1.9

Borat 1.7

Anchorman 1.6

American Pie 1.5

Bridesmaids 1.4

Shaun of the Dead 1.3

Life of Brian 1.2

Compare that to the top five most watched TED talks of all time, at the time of the research being done:

7 Funny and Informative TED Talks:

Mary Roach: 10 things you didn't know about orgasm—3.4 laughs/minute

Seth Godin: This is broken—3.4 laughs/minute

Maysoon Zayid: I got 99 problems … palsy is just one—4 laughs/minute

Ken Robinson: Do schools kill creativity?—2.8 laughs/minute

Shawn Achor: The happy secret to better work—2.9 laughs/minute

Julia Sweeney: It's time for "The Talk"—4.6 laughs/minute

Bob Mankoff: Anatomy of a New Yorker cartoon—2.9 laughs/minute

That's a pretty clear correlation that if you have a message worth sharing, humour is going to create virality.

I have read and studied some of the funniest speakers and entertainers in the world to try and figure out what separates them from the rest. The best strategies I have learnt were from David Nihill and his book, "Do You Talk Funny?".

Ironically, David was absolutely terrified of public speaking himself. Instead of letting it cripple him though, he did the polar opposite. He decided to do hundreds of standup comedy gigs over a 12 month period. Talk about baptism by fire.

When I interviewed David on my Public Speaking Secrets Podcast, we discovered we were both big fans of Tim Ferriss, and in particular the 80/20 rule. What 80/20 rules do you follow to become a humorous speaker?

Your dad jokes have no place there. Stick with real-life experiences when it comes to jokes in your talks. Change your mindset from a knock-knock, why did the chicken cross the road type humour, to one where you turn your everyday experiences, likes, and stories into something that is funny.

Comedians are some of the best storytellers that grace the microphone and for good reason.

Before we jump into those reasons, I want you to put the book down and write down or record yourself telling a funny story. It may be one you use in your talks, one you tell around the water cooler at work, or your go-to at the pub on a Friday night. Deliver it how you would if I walked in the room now and asked you to tell it to me straight off the cuff.

We are now going to use this story to reflect upon and modify as we go through the rest of this chapter. Keeping a funny file is a brilliant way to keep track of all the funny situations we encounter every day. This allows those who don't think they are funny to have a limitless list of stories at their disposal. We need to learn how to trim the fat. Not ab-blaster 3000 fat, but all the edges around your story that aren't needed. The funniest stories are those that are sharp, concise, and get to funny fast. To do this you need to break your story into three parts the intro, setup, and punchline.

The intro should be short and just give enough information to set the scene in the mind of your audience.

The setup is a chance for some misdirection and intrigue. Your audience wants to be in control of the narrative and think they know where it's going.

The punchline is obviously the punchline. Great comedians follow a rule of three when it comes to creating a good punchline. That is, generating three funny parts in the punchline, with the third getting the loudest laugh of all. With the audience already buying into the first part, the laugh will generally build, and by the third part of the punchline, you will have the crowd in stitches.

The transcript below is from Shannon Yarbrough (www.shannonyarbrough.com); a standup comedian and writer who demonstrates how he turns his long form stories into concise and funny stories using the intro, setup, and punchline. He even incorporates the rule of three.

Longform:

I was walking my dog the other day. It was a Tuesday. He's a Collie. He has a purple leash and wakes me up every morning by getting the leash and bringing it to bed and putting it in my hand. He's quite big and always tugs on the leash so it's more like he's walking me. Everywhere we go kids yell out, "Look, Mom, it's Lassie!" I just smile and wave at them. My dog's name is Ralph. It's kind of like if you got mistaken for a celebrity everywhere you go, maybe not a very good celebrity either, like Honey Boo Boo or someone like that. We think Lassie is a good celebrity but maybe dogs hated Lassie. I always imagine Ralph yelling back, "Hey! Fuck you, kid!" Ralph probably hates when people do that but he just smiles and we walk on like we didn't hear them. If I fell down a well, Ralph would probably just pick up my cell phone and call 911 and then play Candy Crush until help arrived.

Revised Version:

The Intro: I was walking my dog the other day. His name is Ralph. He's a Collie.

The Setup: Everywhere we go kids yell out, "Look, it's Lassie!" It's like if you got mistaken for a celebrity, maybe not a very good celebrity either, like Honey Boo Boo. We think Lassie is a good celebrity, but maybe dogs hate Lassie.

The Punchline: I always imagine Ralph yelling back, "Hey! Fuck you, kid!"(Laugh one) If I fell down a well,

Ralph would probably just pick up my cell phone and call 911 (Laugh two) and then play Candy Crush until help arrived. (Laugh three)

You can see in the long form draft there is a lot of superfluous words which takes it longer to get to the punchline. We aren't going to start memorizing your stories word for word but it's important to flesh your stories out and realise where the fluff and where the meat is in each story.

Over time, and the more your deliver it, you will learn where the laugh line is, what works and what doesn't, and you will also start to get a read on the audience as to where they drop out of your stories. Each time, review and restructure it, and eventually, you will be knocking their socks off.

Here's an oxymoron for you; get to the funny fast, but delay the funny.

In practical terms, this means leaving the funny part of your punchline until the end of the sentence. If the funny part of your story is to do with a baby, don't say the baby was in the car; rather say in the car was the baby. This keeps people in suspense and stops everyone laughing while you are still mid-sentence.

Barack Obama highlighted how this can be done in the most formal occasions when addressing senate and world leaders.

We live and do business in the information age, but the last major reorganization of the government happened in the age of black and white TV. There are 12 different agencies that deal with exports. There are at least five different agencies that deal with housing policy. Then there's my favourite example. The interior department is in charge of salmon while they're in fresh water, but the Commerce Department handles them when they're in salt water. I hear it gets even more complicated once they're smoked.

Not all humour in your presentations needs a full story. One way to keep the mode light and your audience engaged is to compare and contrast things that are the complete opposite.

"Asking them to tender this job without a fixed timeline or budget is about as effective as handing a MacBook to a sheep."

Will all humour, and particularly the compare and contrast technique, use images and memes to add to the joke. Often what you are saying may not even be that funny, but when combined with a picture or visual aid, it can change the whole context.

When I run sales webinars I often get to a point before going into the sales stack where I say "Look, I know with all of this new information, it can feel like drinking water out of a fire hydrant...". By itself, it isn't very funny. Combine it with a picture of a young child getting blasted while trying to drink the water, and it changes everything.

With all of the techniques and styles, you are going to now use when you are front and centre of attention, it's important to remember one last thing.

Pause and let them laugh. Give your audience the permission to laugh. You have gone to the effort of making them laugh; now let them.

Chapter 25: The Importance Of Public

Speaking

What Is Public Speaking?

So far we've discussed the fear of public speaking. But what is this thing so many people fear? We generally think of public speaking as standing behind a lectern in front of an audience in a large auditorium. Obviously, there is that sort of situation, but many times the audience is small. Many times you might be responsible to talking to your colleagues or member of your religious organization. You might be addressing a service organization like the Lions Club, for instance.

And though we don't usually think of the following as involving public speakers, they really are. Teachers and professors certainly speak in front of a group of people, as do trial attorneys, or clergymen. So do people at community meetings.

Public speaking may even be talking to no more than three or four people in describing a work problem or to give them information. However, most often we think of speaking in public as giving a speech, whether impromptu—that is, spur of the moment— or prepared. And most often, of course, this is a prepared presentation before a group of people who are there to listen.

There are many reasons for giving speeches. The three most often cited are to inform, to persuade or motivate, and to entertain. Another category often listed is a speech to demonstrate. But this is really a sub-category of a speech to inform, except that it takes things a little further in showing or teaching the audience how to do something—maybe to learn how to use a computer program or how to prepare a certain type of food.

Most often, when we think of professional speakers, those who give motivational talks usually come to mind.

The overall theme generally involves improving an aspect of your life: how to be successful, how to live a more healthful life, and so on.

Around election time you are likely to hear many speeches of persuasion: "My candidate is best, and here's why." Many speeches have the purpose of inspiring the audience to do something, e.g., graduation speeches.

Speeches at public events often are to provide information: Here's what you need to know about changes in the city government, for example. You're likely to hear speeches to entertain at social events—weddings, for instance, or birthday parties.

There are many benefits for a person who is good at giving speeches. Some of them are that public speaking builds self-confidence. It can help in career advancement. It helps your organize your thoughts and get to the point you want to make. It can lead to a career in many different areas.

Why Did You Choose to be a Public Speaker?

Some questions you need to answer now are:

Why do you want to become a public speaker? Is this because you've volunteered or been nominated to give a particular speech? Is it because you want to conquer your fear of addressing groups of people? Is it to succeed at a job? Is it because you're one of those rare people who live to appear in front of others?

If you plan to continue speaking to audiences, you need to determine why. What are your goals? Along with the questions above, think about what skills or personality traits you have that can be assets. Maybe you're a very outgoing person and simply love talking to others. Maybe you have an excellent speaking voice. Once you determine and then work to improve your strongest attributes—and everyone has some—you're already partway to your goal.

Conclusion

There you have it: A casual primer to not being awful in front of a crowd. Hopefully there were some helpful topics — I know that I rarely see a presentation that doesn't have at least some aspect of one of these issues in it, so you can probably be safe in figuring that if you pay attention to the majority of the discussion points raised here, that you've already leapt ahead of many of the people that you might see giving presentations.

The downside is, once you start paying attention to all the little bad behaviors and practices that you know you should improve upon, it becomes much harder to not notice them in other lectures, presentations, and speeches that you sit as an audience member for. Fortunately, the good news is that once you're doing that, chances are decent that you've already become much more self-aware in your own presentations and experiences while speaking in public. The bad news obviously being that within five minutes of a particularly bad speaker, you are actively looking for ways to bludgeon yourself unconscious so you can skip the torture and wake up happily several hours later, with only a concussion-induced headache as your happy reminder that you successfully avoided one of the infinite numbers of poor casual presenters out there.

Public speaking doesn't have to be anything to fear. After I started teaching, I realized I actually really enjoyed it. I started out seeking opportunities to give training at the fire department when they asked for volunteers and later was certified as a CPR instructor. If there was a request in the Reserves to give training during a drill weekend, I'd happily do so (until re-remembering the hours of preparation it takes beyond the 40 minutes of actual speaking required). During annual business conferences and summits, I have no issue learning a topic on the agenda and presenting it. I've realized that each time I get up in front of an audience to talk about a topic that I haven't presented on before (common enough in situations that aren't from a normal, recurring course), I'm still just a bit anxious beforehand. It disappears as soon I start, but the part of me that's trying to make sure I remember all my notes, have my opening down, and am paying attention to the feel of the audience is still going through my mind up until the presentation begins. For me personally, audience size isn't the factor that determines the nervousness level — it's more comfortable to give a lecture I've done before to a group of 90 people than it is to present a topic for the first time to a group of 10. However, once you've got your thoughts down, you're prepared, and you're in tune with some of the ideas presented here, you just might start looking for opportunities to get up in front of the crowd yourself...if only because you don't want to subject yourself and others to the typical amateurish presentation, and you know you have the capability to do it better than the next person.

CPSIA information can be obtained
at www.ICGtesting.com
Printed in the USA
BVHW032212071222
653746BV00010B/80